NS OF DALEKS

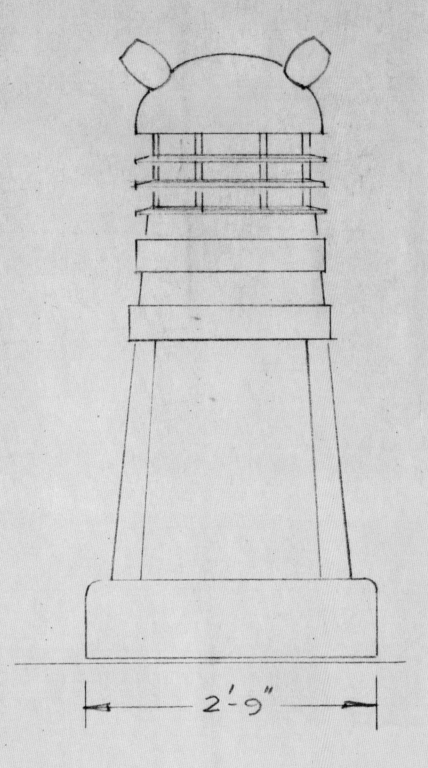

2'-9"

2′-9″

DR. WHO & THE DALEKS

THE OFFICIAL STORY OF THE FILMS

DR. WHO & THE DALEKS

THE OFFICIAL STORY OF THE FILMS

For three little princesses:
Charlotte, Annabel & Helena

ISBN: 9781803360188
Ebook ISBN: 9781803360898

Published by
Titan Books
A division of Titan Publishing Group Ltd
144 Southwark St
London
SE1 0UP

www.titanbooks.com

First edition: September 2022

2 4 6 8 10 9 7 5 3 1

Did you enjoy this book? We love to hear from our readers.
Please e-mail us at: readerfeedback@titanemail.com or
write to Reader Feedback at the above address.

To receive advance information, news, competitions, and exclusive
offers online, please sign up for the Titan newsletter on our website:
www.titanbooks.com

A CIP catalogue record for this title is available from the British Library.

Printed and bound in China.

DR. WHO & THE DALEKS

THE OFFICIAL STORY OF THE FILMS

JOHN WALSH

TITANBOOKS

CONTENTS

6 FOREWORDS

FOREWORDS

Little did I know when director Gordon Flemyng came to my school for a mass audition for the part that it would have set me on this path. There were no script lines to read, just a friendly chat. Then, a few weeks later, I got a call to go to Shepperton Film Studios for a screen test.

I remember watching *Doctor Who* on television with William Hartnell and Carole Ann Ford as Susan. So I was thrilled that they were making this big colour feature film, and that I'd got the part. Luckily, I already had some experience acting in films with *High Wind in Jamaica* (1965), starring Anthony Quinn and the Children's Film Foundation.

Peter Cushing was lovely to me. He became a surrogate grandfather when we were working. The other actors said he

had never worked with children before. Peter liked the fact that my Susan was intelligent for her years. She had helped her grandfather build the TARDIS, and he was teaching her everything; she was not just a typical 11-year-old. He even made sure I was signed up for the sequel before he agreed to take part.

I didn't realise how big the films would be until I went to open stores in Birmingham and Manchester as part of the film's publicity tour. When we drove into the town centre, there were thousands of children with their parents queuing up to see the display of Daleks. Only then did I realise how successful *Doctor Who* was. I got lots of letters asking for photographs, and I also got a chance to record a song. Having the opportunity to do something like that was tremendous, all by the time I was twelve!

The Daleks captured everybody's imagination. The show scared the life out of the children, who would be peering from behind the settee but wouldn't turn it off. I don't think anyone realised what a success they had on their hands. Its unique blend of fantasy and drama has made it endure for 60 years, and I'm thrilled to be a small part of that. Sometimes I worry that the feature films get forgotten, but then I see the fans' great affection for them; I am sure Peter would be thrilled to see how much the public still loves him as Dr. Who.

I'm delighted that you will finally read the full story in John Walsh's book.

—ROBERTA TOVEY

Since I can remember, I've known about the Daleks. The original film posters were framed on our walls, and my brother and I always puffed out our chests when we were described as "the sons of the guy who made those Dalek movies." The guy was Gordon Flemyng. He's the reason I thought a life in film was possible and obtainable. Dad was obsessed with film, storytelling, and the magic of the film set. Like father, like son – and the posters are still on the wall.

Driving down Sunset Boulevard in LA, I had never felt closer to him, knowing he had driven the same streets alone and pursued a film career. It was like I could feel him, and as I drove into studios for auditions, I would whisper, "Here we go, Dad." My dad's career made my career a possibility, not a fantasy – as the son of a policeman thinks about joining the force, a lawyer's kid might join the bar, or the doctor's son might consider doing the same. The Doctor!

—JASON FLEMYNG

DR. WHO & THE DALEKS : THE OFFICIAL STORY OF THE FILMS

INTRODUCTION

OPPOSITE: Peter Cushing leads his cast, Roberta Tovey, Jennie Linden & Roy Castle, outside Shepperton Studios Stage H. Colourisation by Clayton Hickman

BELOW: Daleks get some workplace supervision from their leaders.

RIGHT: A restored Dalek from the *Invasion Earth* sequel.

Doctor Who has become a television institution since its launch in 1963. For decades it has been the mainstay family drama that has brought millions of people together for Saturday early evening viewing. Through time and space and a variety of actors regenerating in the role, the monsters, the space ship, and the eccentric and mysterious time-travelling figure of the Doctor have kept the front pages of British newspapers fascinated for six decades; and it shows no signs of coming to an end, after 862 episodes and an audience estimated to be over 100 million worldwide. The Doctor's iconic nemeses the Daleks have kept the Time Lord busy through the years – and never more so than when they made their big screen debut in 1965.

George Pal's 1960 big-screen adaptation of H.G. Wells' *The Time Machine*, featuring an intrepid time traveller and female companion, had been an enormous success with audiences; it was also a big influence on the BBC's newly appointed Head of Drama, the Canadian-born Sydney Newman. He had been brought in to the BBC in 1961 to shake up the bleak and staid image of the department, and although other drama writers Donald Wilson and C. E. Webber fleshed out the characters and storylines, it was Newman's vision to have a time traveller called the Doctor whose time machine was larger on the inside than outside.

There was little enthusiasm for the series within the BBC, and both of Newman's first picks to run the series, producers Don Taylor and later Shaun Sutton, turned it down. It would be Newman's former production assistant at ABC Television, Verity Lambert, who would get the Doctor off and running for his first adventures in space and time. She became the BBC's first female drama producer.

Doctor Who had been on television screens for a year and a half by the time the first feature film, *Dr. Who & The Daleks*, premièred. The film divided fans for many years; Peter Cushing's performance is only loosely based on the character of the first on-screen portrayal of the Doctor, by William Hartnell. But it would not be until late 1969 that the BBC launched its first full-colour television service, and even then it would not be until January 1972 that Jon Pertwee's Doctor would confront his mortal enemy in 'Day of the Daleks'. Whatever their opinion on the faithfulness of the big-screen adaptation, fans of the Daleks decided this would not deter them from seeing them for the first time in colour – and in widescreen Techniscope.

By 1965 "Dalekmania" was at its height, the Daleks having been introduced on television in 1963. The *Dr. Who* film of 1965 and the sequel in 1966 benefited from that wave of that hysteria. Once the mania for all things Dalek had subsided, the films, too, had become distant memories for many cinema-goers. Fans over the years argued that Peter Cushing's Dr. Who was not an official part of the *Doctor Who* legend; it was an unofficial side path and should not be recognised as part of the accepted timeline. It was simply not 'canon'. In defence of the films, they were made before the first time that the Doctor 'regenerated', into Patrick Troughton in November 1966. Hartnell's Doctor never had clearly established his origins: especially that he was not even an Earthling at all.

In subsequent years many tried and failed to make a big-screen adventure for the Time Lord. The fourth Doctor, Tom Baker, attempted this with a script he penned with fellow cast member Ian Marter, entitled 'Scratchman'. But the legacy of the 1960s film adaptations endured. In 2014 the then-*Doctor Who* showrunner Steven Moffat (2009-2017) outed himself as Peter Cushing film devotee:

"When I started writing [the 50th Anniversary special] 'The Day of the Doctor', I knew I wanted every Doctor to make some sort of appearance [...] But what about Peter

OPPOSITE TOP: Bernard Cribbins enters the white doors of the TARDIS and is greeted by Peter Cushing, whilst Roberta Tovey works on a new experiment.

OPPOSITE BELOW: Dr. Who examines the Thal's Dalek City map on Skaro.

BELOW: A press call photoshoot for the Thal actors, led by Barrie Ingham, second from left.

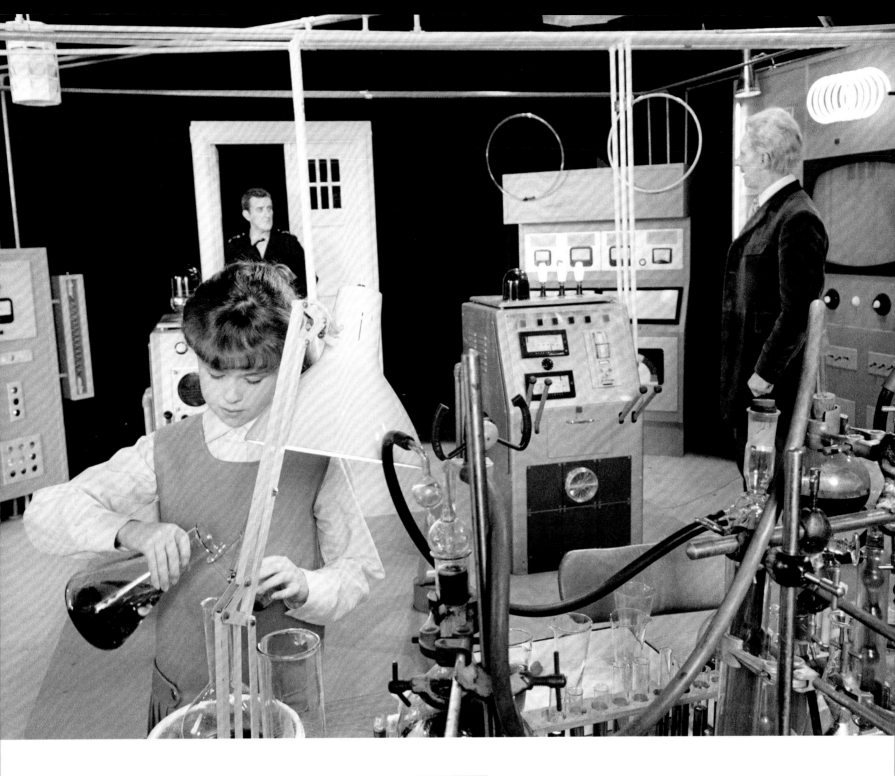

Cushing?! Now, I love those movies, and I don't care if you beat me up in the playground because they got *Doctor Who* wrong – they're fun and funny, with great Daleks and a terrific Doctor. But they don't exactly fit with the rest of the show, do they?"

In a further nod of approval and acceptance, when *Doctor Who* made its triumphant return to screens in 2005 after a break of sixteen years, the newly designed TARDIS bore the same white-accented police box design from the second film, *Daleks' Invasion Earth 2150 A.D.*

1965 was the year of the epic motion picture. The top three films were James Bond's fourth outing *Thunderball*, David Lean's wintry saga *Doctor Zhivago* and, in the top spot, musical extravaganza *The Sound of Music*. Of the nearly 3,000 films released worldwide in 1965, few are being talked about and restored in high definition today. However, *Dr. Who & The Daleks* and its sequel have endured due to an audience

appreciation for the films and the *Doctor Who*'s fan base's fascination with the unconventional history of this continually intriguing Time Lord.

For this book, I was granted access to all materials in the vast StudioCanal archive, including unseen high-resolution photography, film elements and rare documents. For the first time these precious Time Lord relics have been given a 21st Century restoration by Clayton Hickman, whose work you will see throughout this book. Clayton has not recoloured the past. Instead, he has returned the photos to their original colour state, as much of the on-set photography, by Ted Reed for the first film, and Bert Cann for the sequel, was shot on colour negative film. Additional portrait photography from the first film was by George Konig.

The photos would have been printed black and white on 8x10 photographic paper for newspapers and general publicity. This black and white material remains, whilst the original colour camera negative no longer exists. Clayton has allowed us all to go back in time to 1965 and 1966 to see what the on-set photographers, known as Unit Stills, would have seen during the production of the films. Our collective thanks to Mr Hickman, a true time-traveller.

The first multi-layered Dalek set for the sequel, *Invasion Earth*.

Newly discovered and restored images from the StudioCanal archive.

Press photoshoot with Roberta Tovey for the first film, flanked by new shinier and taller Daleks.

DALEK NATION

Doctor Who's launch episode on 23 November 1963 was a mixture of contemporary time travel and prehistoric melodrama. Public reaction was muted, and while the show's debut had understandably been overshadowed by the assassination of the American President, John F. Kennedy, the previous day, low ratings of six million viewers suggested this might be a short-lived series. However, the following story, by a young writer called Terry Nation, was entitled 'Dead Planet', and introduced the world to the Daleks. By the end of the seven-week run, ratings were over 10.5 million.

Welsh-born Nation got his first professional writing break, on radio comedy, for Spike Milligan, Eric Sykes and Frankie Howerd in 1955. Milligan had bought his first comedy sketch, saying he thought the writer 'looked hungry'. Nation's first major television writing commission would be for Tony Hancock's ITV series in 1963. He had initially turned down an offer from scriptwriter David Whitaker to write for *Doctor Who*, but at age

33, when the costs of his new young family began to press, he took on the second story for William Hartnell's Doctor, and the Daleks were born. The first Dalek serial was initially entitled 'The Survivors.' This would then change to 'The Mutants' during production, and the title was kept through to broadcast.

Growing up during the Second World War shaped Nation's storytelling. He based the Daleks on the Nazis and their obsession with conquest at any price. The 'Dalek Invasion of Earth' television serial in 1964 bears this parallel out most vividly. Nation was keen to move away from the science fiction staple of a man in a monster suit. His inventive but straightforward concept, that his Daleks would have no legs and glide like the long-skirted dancers of the Georgian National Ballet, would cement the legacy of the alien invaders.

It fell to in-house BBC designer Raymond Cusick to build the full-size Daleks. Cusick came up with concept art in less than an hour, inspired by his initial sketches of a pepper pot

OPPOSITE: Terry Nation in December 1964 with his iconic Daleks from the first television story.

BELOW: In 1973 Allan Ballard was commissioned by *Radio Times* to photograph Terry Nation at home for *Doctor Who*'s Tenth Anniversary Special.

FROM THE BBC TELEVISION SERIAL BY
TERRY NATION

on a table. This was only to give an idea of the basic design. He originally wanted a much more complex looking machine but was limited to a budget of just £60 (approximately £1,000 today). Cusick knew he needed someone inside to operate it, so designed it to the scale of a seated man.

Despite his iconic design being seen the world over, no royalties would be paid to Cusick because of his status as permanent in-house staff within the BBC. However, Terry Nation held onto the story rights for his metal monsters. Nation would write or approve all future stories for the Daleks and would benefit financially from the wave of popularity that spin-off merchandise would generate. His estate continues to approve all commercial Dalek projects and protects their legacy.

In 1987 Nation told *Doctor Who Magazine* that he recognised Cusick's "tremendous contribution" to the Dalek design. "Cusick didn't get anything, to my understanding. I think they may have given him a hundred-pound bonus, but he was a salaried employee, and I think he knew the nature of his work, and it was what he did every week. The copyrights resided with the BBC and myself, so that before they could merchandise anything, they had to have my agreement. I was very lucky."

By the time of the first motion picture, *Dr. Who & The Daleks*, Nation was in high demand on other projects and asked a trusted colleague to keep an eye on his valuable assets. In an interview from the documentary *Dalekmania*, Terry Nation explained, "I went to a couple of meetings, at the beginning. But by this time, I was absorbed into doing something else. And I asked David Whitaker to translate my television screenplay into the screenplay for cinema."

Nation was not critical of colleague Whitaker's work but did question the performance of the leading actor Peter Cushing. "With *Dr. Who & The Daleks*, I was giving it away at this point. I'd done that story, my name was going to be over it anyway, it was all going to be based on my work, and David Whitaker was eager to do it, so that's what we did. I would have gone back very much closer to the thing we did on television. I've seen those first seven episodes, and they are really good. They are very well-constructed. I thought Peter Cushing played the Doctor very well. I would have liked to have seen a little more snap, but he was very loveable, and that's the way he wanted to play it.

ABOVE LEFT: Terry Nation and Raymond Cusick in 1964 posing with a TV Dalek.

ABOVE RIGHT: Cusick inspects his creations.

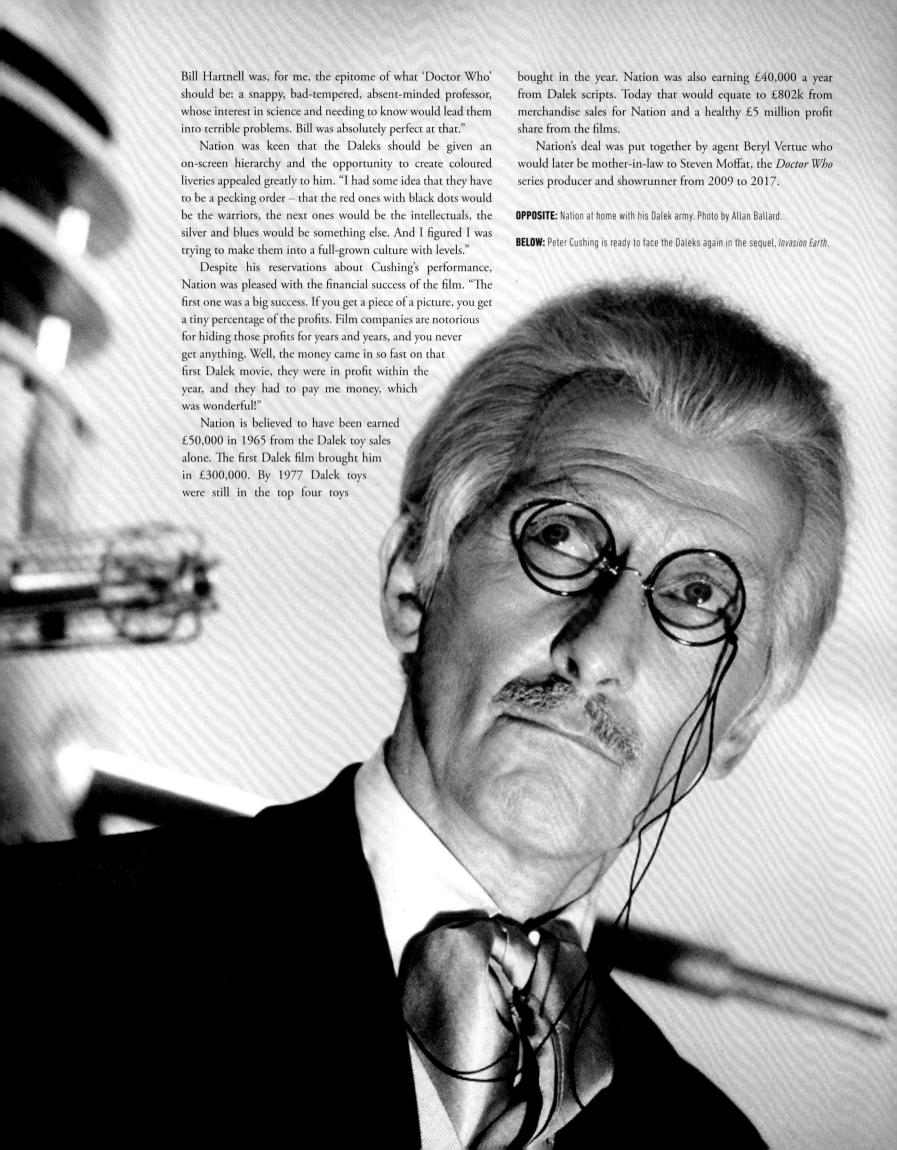

Bill Hartnell was, for me, the epitome of what 'Doctor Who' should be: a snappy, bad-tempered, absent-minded professor, whose interest in science and needing to know would lead them into terrible problems. Bill was absolutely perfect at that."

Nation was keen that the Daleks should be given an on-screen hierarchy and the opportunity to create coloured liveries appealed greatly to him. "I had some idea that they have to be a pecking order – that the red ones with black dots would be the warriors, the next ones would be the intellectuals, the silver and blues would be something else. And I figured I was trying to make them into a full-grown culture with levels."

Despite his reservations about Cushing's performance, Nation was pleased with the financial success of the film. "The first one was a big success. If you get a piece of a picture, you get a tiny percentage of the profits. Film companies are notorious for hiding those profits for years and years, and you never get anything. Well, the money came in so fast on that first Dalek movie, they were in profit within the year, and they had to pay me money, which was wonderful!"

Nation is believed to have been earned £50,000 in 1965 from the Dalek toy sales alone. The first Dalek film brought him in £300,000. By 1977 Dalek toys were still in the top four toys

bought in the year. Nation was also earning £40,000 a year from Dalek scripts. Today that would equate to £802k from merchandise sales for Nation and a healthy £5 million profit share from the films.

Nation's deal was put together by agent Beryl Vertue who would later be mother-in-law to Steven Moffat, the *Doctor Who* series producer and showrunner from 2009 to 2017.

OPPOSITE: Nation at home with his Dalek army. Photo by Allan Ballard.

BELOW: Peter Cushing is ready to face the Daleks again in the sequel, *Invasion Earth*.

DALEKMANIA

OPPOSITE: The Rolykins Daleks from 1965. Photos from Christopher Hill / The Space Museum.

BELOW: Tie-in publications and a rare advertisement for the Codeg Dalek. Photos from Mick Hall.

GENESIS OF THE DALEKS MERCHANDISE

The explosion of public affection for, and obsession with, the metal monsters was comparable only to The Beatles. Nothing like it from film or television had been seen before. The touchpaper had been lit on a world of merchandise, from toys and records to books, comics and plans for three feature films. Unusually, licences for the same Dalek product lines were given to a variety of different companies. Newspapers and magazines were full of the exploits of the Daleks after their impressive debut serial – seven episodes on television from 21 December 1963 to 1 February 1964. However, it took until late 1965 to complete the licensing deals and task toy manufacturers with quenching the audience's thirst for anything that even slightly resembled a Dalek.

1/8 Dr. Who "Dodge the Daleks" Boxed Game
117/22 The Mysterious Clockwork "Dalek" Figure
36/2 The Plastic "Dalek" Money Bank

All trade enquiries to :-

COWAN, de GROOT LTD
WAKEFIELD HOUSE, CHART ST, LONDON N.I

Marx Toys were first with their 4.5-inch-high plastic Dalek toy. The earliest versions were friction-driven. Later models were battery-operated and featured a bumping mechanism that allowed them to hit the wall, turn, and continue their domination of children's bedrooms. These were sold at pocket money prices, but today a mint Louis Marx Dalek in a box could set you back as much as £400. The toys were even used by visual effects technicians in place of the actual on-screen Daleks for model shots.

Several companies were permitted licences to make toys. Codeg's wind-up Dalek was given life with a few simple turns of a key. Made in fewer numbers, these are highly sought-after by collectors. Other toys included board games and a kite. There was even a full-size Dalek that you could wear: part tent, part raincoat. Scorpion Automotives's Northampton factory manufactured the Berwick Dalek playsuit; unfortunately, most of the stock was destroyed by a fire, and the remaining few are considered the holy grail of Dalek memorabilia.

The smallest and most successful of all the Dalek toys must be the one-inch-tall Dalek Rolykins. A simple hollow plastic body had a small ball bearing inside for gliding along the floor. Priced at just one shilling, or around five pence today, this tiny Dalek is estimated to have sold over a million by the end of 1965.

The Daleks were still ruling the airwaves too. Their creator Terry Nation recalled, "I remember with great pride that the commercial channel was running the Beatles when they were really at their peak, at the same time as a *Doctor Who* episode with the Daleks, and *Doctor Who* got the ratings. I was pretty pleased with that."

ABOVE LEFT: Louis Marx friction Dalek.

ABOVE RIGHT: Codeg's clockwork Dalek.

LEFT: The highly sought-after Berwick Playsuit. All photos on this page are from Christopher Hill / The Space Museum.

RESURRECTION OF THE DALEKS MERCHANDISE

In 2005, the most realistic Dalek toys ever seen by the eager eyes of fans invaded shops, from Steve Walker's Product Enterprise. These impressive 12-inch remote-controlled Daleks came in three colours: standard silver, red and black. They also spoke original Dalek dialogue from the film's soundtrack. The remote control was a mini version of the Dalek saucer. They retailed at £29.99, but today you can expect to pay upwards of £200. An ultra-rare limited edition of 1,000 made in a chrome effect would be worth £500 today. Not only were they as accurate as anything on Skaro, but they also had packing design by legendary movie poster artist Graham Humphries, who has kindly allowed me to reproduce his original art here. Others amongst this range included a remote-controlled inflatable 48-inch Dalek, a remake of the Codeg clockwork edition from 1965, the mini Rolykin Dalek and a four-pack set of 2½-inch 'micro' talking *Invasion Earth* Daleks in four colours.

RIGHT: All Daleks Product Enterprise photos from Steve Walker.

BELOW: Graham Humphries' artwork magnificently reimagines London under siege by the invading Dalek army.

The latest invaders of the merchandising landscape are 2019's Character Options with their boxed pair of Daleks from TV serial 'The Chase'. Two movie Daleks from the first film were used in a fleeting scene, and whilst these models are packaged as television Daleks the big-screen design is unmistakable. These six-inch toys are called the Jungles of Mechanus Daleks, and retailed for £29.99 in 2020. They sold out within weeks and prices are close to £100 today.

TOP: Graham Humphries' artwork for the inflatable and infrared-controlled Daleks.

ABOVE: The most recent additions to the Dalek family, from Character Options.

FROM SMALL SCREEN TO BIG SCREEN

OPPOSITE: Milton Subotsky ensconced in his office with science fiction and fantasy books. Photo from Dr Fiona Subotsky.

Horror filmmakers Amicus had bought an option to make two previously televised *Doctor Who* drama series into feature films. Concern that family audiences might be deterred from a *Doctor Who* film by the Amicus name, and the need for co-financing, lead to a partnership with producer Joe Vegoda and his company Aaru Productions. Amicus' driving force was an American producer and writer, Milton Subotsky. His confident and sure-footed rewriting of the elderly time traveller and his metal enemies would prove box office dynamite.

Subotsky's base was at Shepperton Studios, where he produced his films, most notably horror anthologies like *Dr Terror's House of Horrors* (1965). It starred Peter Cushing and was directed by Freddie Francis, his proposed dream team for the first *Doctor Who* film. (Subotsky's 1974 compendium *The Vault of Horror* would feature future Doctor Tom Baker). Subotsky secured the rights for the *Doctor Who* feature films for just £500.

Along with producing partner Max Rosenberg, he offered an alternative to the more lurid Hammer Horror films. The *Guardian* obituary for Subotsky tried to clarify the difference between the two horror film companies. "Amicus films were typically brooding and claustrophobic; they were far darker, and much less camp than the horror films of the same period produced by the more famous Hammer studios." It is believed that Subotsky saw Hammer as more than mere rivals; Hammer had rejected an early script he had written in 1956, entitled *Frankenstein and the Monster*, but later made a version with many similar themes, *The Curse of Frankenstein* (1957).

By the mid-1960s, Subotsky and Rosenberg were looking for larger, family audiences, and *Doctor Who* was the perfect vehicle for them. This would only be the second time a British television series had translated to the cinema screen. The first was the 1955 release of *The Quatermass Xperiment*, based on the six-part television series from 1953, the correctly spelt *The Quatermass Experiment*. 1970s cinema audiences would see a wave of popular television series made into colour feature films, mostly based on situation comedies: *Till Death Us Do Part* (1969), *Up Pompeii* (1971), *Steptoe and Son* (1972), *The Likely Lads* (1976) and *Porridge* (1979). Hammer Films hit box-office gold when their debut cinematic outing for ITV's *On the Buses* (1971) made more at the UK box office that year than the highly anticipated return of Sean Connery as James Bond in *Diamonds Are Forever*.

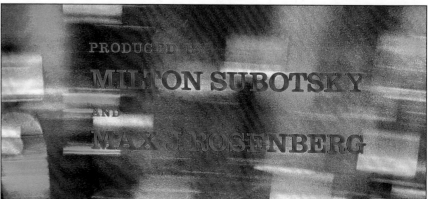

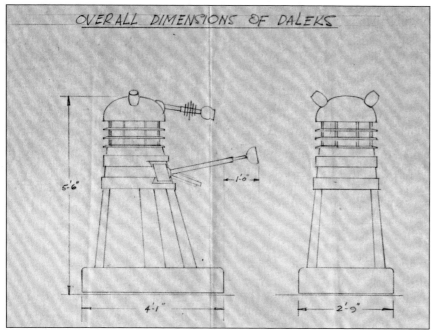

OVERALL DIMENSIONS OF DALEKS

5'-6"   1'-0"
4'-1"   2'-9"

TOP: Subotsky & Vegoda. Photo from Marcus Brooks / The UK Peter Cushing Appreciation Society.

ABOVE: Early Dalek drawing from Subotsky's personal collection. The artist was never identified. Photo from Richard Holliss.

New York-born Subotsky had made technical training films when he served in the Signal Corps during World War II. After working in US television on the TV series *Junior Science* he moved to England in 1959. He would find his feet as a producer of horror feature films, with *The City of the Dead* (a.k.a. *Horror Hotel*, 1960). Because of his musical abilities, he was asked to be a regular juror on the BBC Television series *Juke Box Jury* in the early 1960s. For his first feature film *Rock, Rock, Rock* (1956) Subotsky composed nine songs.

In Shepperton, his office was described by journalist Chris Knight for *Cinefantastique* magazine (1973) as "one of six chalets, all identical ... clustered between two sound stages. His desk is littered with papers and telephones, and on the surrounding shelves are, neatly stacked, hundreds of books, magazines, paperbacks and hardcovers, all seemingly connected with horror, fantasy and science fiction."

Subotsky's enthusiasm for cinema was apparent from an early age. He would watch as many as six films each Saturday at his local cinema in Brooklyn, by saving up his lunch money during the week and going without food. His family thought the movie business was disreputable, so he pursued a night school course in engineering. For a day job, he was hired as a camera assistant in documentaries. "I did everything: carry the

camera, load it, walk behind it with the battery. I went into film editing and then started writing scripts."

It was cheaper for Subotsky to make his films in the UK than in the US, but there was more to the story than mere economics. "You can get a marvellous quality here. You have wonderful technicians and a very good pool of actors to choose from," he explained. Rosenberg discovered shooting in the UK to be a perfect financial opportunity, as the Eady plan had been set up to allow filmmakers access to government money to encourage filming in the UK. Between them, Subotsky and Rosenberg claimed to read five hundred novels a year in their search to find the perfect film idea.

"Rosenberg, who was the money man, was always in America, and we never met him," says Ingrid Pitt, the Polish-born actor who starred with *Doctor Who*'s Jon Pertwee as a sultry vampire in *The House That Dripped Blood*. "But Milton was an angel. He was often on set, and he had a way of making you feel wanted. We used to sit around and talk about medicine. He always thought he had something wrong with him."

Given the many differences between the *Doctor Who* television series and the two films, Subotsky summed up his rapid-fire approach to storytelling when discussing the television screening of the sequel *Daleks' Invasion Earth 2150 AD*. "It still looks good today. The sets were good. The plot was a bit hard

ABOVE LEFT: William Hartnell's Doctor's first encounter with the Daleks.

ABOVE RIGHT: Hartnell at the TARDIS door in the pilot episode 'An Unearthly Child' (1963). Colourisation by Clayton Hickman.

BELOW: The backlot street set at Shepperton Studios for the Dalek sequel *Invasion Earth*.

to follow. Dr. Who took twenty seconds to explain what they were doing and then, bang! You were into two reels of action, showing them doing it. If I did it again, I would make the plot a lot clearer. I was worried about boring an audience. My wife thinks I edit my pictures too fast. She tells me if you blink, you might miss an important point."

In an interview with *Kinematography Weekly* in 1965 Subotsky explained how he adapted the show for cinema. "We've taken Terry Nation's first seven episodes of the TV serial and rewritten them into a screenplay, at the same time injecting a considerable amount of comedy. On TV they take themselves so deadly seriously. This is all action, excitement and comedy." Subotsky's ambition for the film was evident in his desire to create a larger screen spectacle. "We intend to make full use of the colour, spectacle and action that make the difference between large and small screen entertainment. One of the things we have to make it different and better is splendour."

Subotsky would return to science fiction with a trio of Edgar Rice Burroughs' stories, *The Land that Time Forgot* (1975), *At the Earth's Core* (1976) – this time with Peter Cushing playing Dr Abner Perry, reprising a variation of his Dr. Who performance – and lastly *The People That Time Forgot* (1977). By the last film, the business relationship with Rosenberg had ended; future projects were solo affairs. These included the television mini-series of Ray Bradbury's *The Martian Chronicles* (1980). Subotsky was the first to option screen rights from new horror writer Stephen King. Several Stephen King film adaptations followed for which Subotsky would receive a contractual producer credit, the last being *The Lawnmower Man* (1992).

BELOW: This newly-discovered image shows the lights and cables used on location for the Bedfordshire mine sequence, which was shot on the Shepperton Studios backlot.

A PARALLEL UNIVERSE

BELOW LEFT: TV Time Lord William Hartnell in 'The Daleks' Master Plan' (1965). Colourisation by Clayton Hickman.

BELOW RIGHT: Movie Time Lord Peter Cushing faces off with a sequel Dalek. Photo from Mick Hall.

The replacement of leading actor William Hartnell in the television series *Doctor Who* would not occur until the end of 1966, when Patrick Troughton would regenerate as the second Doctor. In 1965 William Hartnell was firmly fixed into the minds of viewers as the only Doctor. Peter Cushing's portrayal is a departure, and one which fans have debated for decades. Out goes Hartnell's irascible school headteacher, and in comes Cushing's avuncular and kindly grandfather.

William Hartnell was annoyed at being recast with Peter Cushing as a character he had made a household name. Peter Cushing had 'marquee value', and his name would be known to cinemagoers in America, where the film's producers were hoping to make the films into a franchise. Both actors were playing a

much older man for their respective roles: William Hartnell was 57 years old in 1965 and Cushing 52. Cushing's Doctor appears to be around 70 years old.

Cushing's film companions are his two grandchildren, Susie and Barbara, and Barbara's love interest Ian, played by Roy Castle. The character names were retained from the television series but the roles changed. Originally Barbara and Ian were the schoolteachers of a teenage Susan, who lived with her grandfather, the Doctor. However, screenwriter and producer Milton Subotsky was keen to keep the story as simple and fast-moving as possible, so these changes were made for dramatic convenience rather than to create distance between the two portrayals.

Cushing plays the Doctor as an Earthling, to accommodate American audiences' lack of knowledge of the UK series. In the short term this simplified the narrative, but in the long-term was frowned upon by some viewers and film critics.

Perhaps the most significant argument amongst the loyal viewers of the series is in the name itself. Cushing refers to himself as "Dr. Who." Hartnell never did, only as the Doctor. For the entire run of the classic television series, he would only be known as the Doctor, although occasionally, for dramatic and comedic effect, he called himself Dr John Smith; Patrick Troughton's Doctor claimed the name during an interrogation in 'The War Games' (1969).

Changes to the size and scale of the production are more prominent. Larger Daleks in various colours, a bigger TARDIS exterior, and a more 1960s-style jazz score put the films on another plane from the series. This larger scale was intentional as Subotsky wanted to create something grander than television could achieve. He wanted the audience to have a cinematic experience; and he certainly achieved this. Whichever version of the original time traveller fans prefer, one thing is true: both have withstood the greatest challenge of all – the test of time.

ABOVE LEFT TO RIGHT: Dr. Who with Susan, played by Roberta Tovey for the film, alongside Carol Ann Ford as the television Susan, with Hartnell in the first story 'An Unearthly Child' (1963). Colourisation by Clayton Hickman.

BIG SCREEN DALEKS

LEFT: The Daleks take Manhattan for their press photocall on the backlot street set at Shepperton Studios for the first film. Photo from Mark Wolf.

Doctor Who on television was considered neither cheap nor lacking in technical achievement in 1963; at the time, the series set a new standard for science fiction on television. But Milton Subotsky was a showman, and knew that a cinema audience would demand higher production values than were offered by the television series. Making the transition to the big screen allowed for the introduction of colour for the first time, and a redesign for the now-famous alien overlords, the Daleks.

Eighteen expensive, more detailed Daleks were created for the film. The sink plunger arm from the television series was replaced with a menacing claw arm on some. The use of colour allowed for visual hierarchies, with two Dalek leaders painted red and black respectively. The original television Daleks were five feet high; these big-screen Daleks were an impressive five foot six inches, although press releases state five foot eight inches.

Shawcraft Models was the company commissioned to build the original Dalek props for the television series, so it made sense for the movie Daleks to be manufactured there too. In February 1965 the updated Daleks were created from the original moulds, but they were sleeker, with a high specification for cinema. In addition, they would be more detailed for their big-screen debut, using expensive fibreglass.

FILM DALEKS 1

The most noticeable upgrades for the film Daleks were the oversized base skirt, the wrap-around box for the claw arm, the gun at a steeper angle and higher neck rings. The Dalek eyestalk had five disc rings, and the domed head was topped with much larger lights to signify which machine was talking. Eight Daleks were created for a cost of £350 each. The Plaster Workshops also produced some background Daleks, with less detail, at Shepperton Studios for £100 each.

The Daleks' guns were wider than their TV counterparts, but the debate on the use of fire extinguishers over laser fire still rages today. Subotsky was keen to avoid the high cost of optical effects work, which would have been expensive for a film such as this, with hundreds of individually animated, rendered and photographed lasers coming from the Daleks. Subotsky's adaptations of Edgar Rice Burroughs' *The Land That Time Forgot* (1975) and *At the Earth's Core* (1976) had used front-projection techniques, which allowed the actors to see their monstrous adversaries on set on large screens. It was all filmed in-camera to save on costly post-production optical effects matting.

But Dalek lasers would need to be composited in an optical printer with the original film shot in the studio. A combined element would need to be produced with both the studio footage and the new laser effects. Not only would the costs have been prohibitive, but on the two-perforation Techniscope format, which has half the resolution of four-perforation 35mm anamorphic film, there would be a loss in quality: the image would lose a generation each time an optical effect would be used. Director Gordon Flemyng confirms the financial constraints: "We used [extinguishers] because we couldn't afford to add a ray to the film."

It is also believed that one of Subotsky's ideas for the Dalek guns was refused by the British Board of Film Censors, who deemed it too violent for a general family certification. The BBFC's archive reveals that the "U" certification was granted because: "The Daleks use a kind of gas to knock out their enemies. Although the gas appears to be non-fatal and doesn't seem to cause any lasting injury, it does lead to a sense of mild threat." In an interview with *Kinematography Weekly* in 1965

ABOVE: The Daleks make a big first impression in widescreen.

OPPOSITE: Never-before published image of the Daleks being prepared for filming on Stage H, at Shepperton Studios during the sequel in 1966. Photo from Colin Young.

Subotsky confirmed that more dramatic weapons for the Daleks had been considered. "We were going to have them shooting out flames, but John Trevelyan, the censor, thought children were frightened of flames. So we went to the other extreme and armed them with fire extinguishers!"

Revealing the inside alien that drove each Dalek was also forbidden by the censors, as Flemyng recalled. "No one had ever shown what a Dalek looked like and we decided that it was basically a brain, an intelligence with no recognisable features. I remember going to talk to the censor about what I was going to show when I took the lid off this thing and how I might be able to get round not showing it. Because what the censor was saying was, 'You are not to show it. If you show something and it's a problem to us, we're going to cut it out, because this is a young person's film.'"

There are variations in colour and design among the Daleks. Some have a double-jawed mechanical claw arm, others have the plungers recognised by TV viewers, and a blow torch cuts through an elevator door in the Dalek city. The main 'worker' Daleks are painted silver with blue domes, hemispheres and fenders, and topped off with a gold collar. Shawcraft Models used a technique for hemisphere alignment that was based on the television Dalek which had different dimensions and was shorter than their big screen cousins; once this technique was carried across to the movie Daleks there were some misalignments that ran through the entire population of Dalek City. The Dalek leader's primary colour is black, with alternating silver and gold hemispheres and neck rings. Both collars and base-skirting or fender are gold. The leader's deputy is a red Dalek with black hemispheres and, like the leader, a gold collar and skirt. All of these new versions are topped with red dome lights.

Three of the film Daleks would get a brief cameo appearance to help make up the Dalek numbers on the *Doctor Who* television serial 'The Chase' in 1965. These looked in poor repair, with missing fenders and the larger lights replaced with the smaller television-compliant versions. The first Dalek feature film would be released in August 1965, three months after viewers would have seen them in 'The Chase'. The scene is fleeting, and with no possibility of recording the episode, it is doubtful many viewers would have noticed.

DALEK OPERATORS:

Bruno Castagnoli Kevin Manser
Michael Dillon   Eric McKay
Bryan Hands   Len Saunders
Robert Jewell   Gerald Taylor

DALEK VOICES:

Peter Hawkins
David Graham

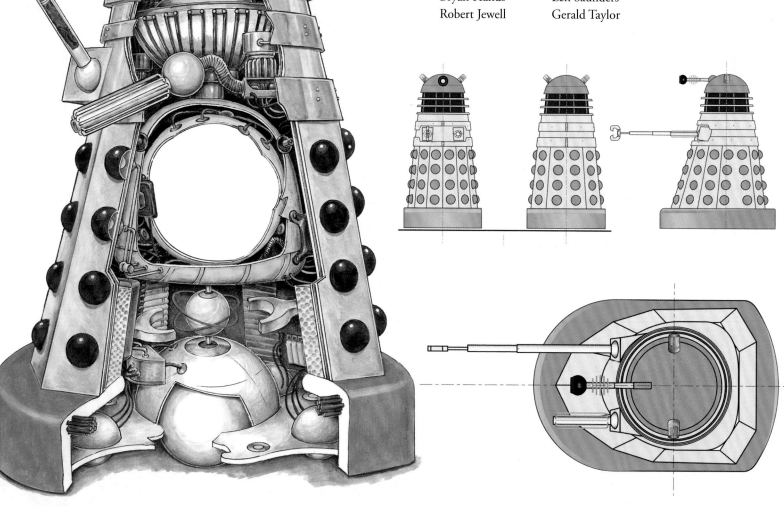

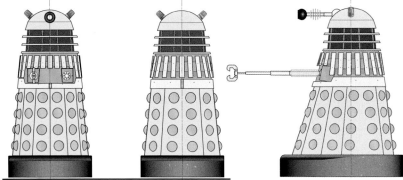

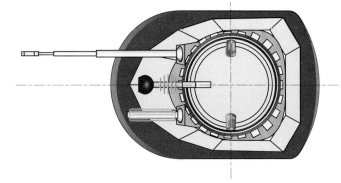

THIS PAGE: Daleks take their marks on the street set at Shepperton. This restored image reveals the chalk line at the base of the Dalek.

RIGHT: Design image by John Darley / Project Dalek.

FILM DALEKS 2

The few Daleks from the first film that were retained for the sequel had been either damaged, given away in competitions or were on a worldwide publicity tour for the first film. A solution to an instant Dalek army was to be found in an unlikely place. A new stage play, *The Curse of the Daleks*, was running at the Wyndham Theatre. Five new Daleks had been made for the production by Shawcraft Models. These were added to the sequel Daleks to boost their on-screen numbers.

There were some modifications to the designs for the sequel, including the addition of an upper collar mesh and wrap-around metal slats in line with the traditional television Dalek. A variant on the Daleks' attachments include a smaller silver plunger in place of the usual black item, and a scissor claw. Many of these Daleks ended up being given away as competition prizes. It is believed Terry Nation bought some, including the theatre's versions, and one ended up in Jon Pertwee's 1973 serial 'Planet of the Daleks', retaining the impressive larger dome lights.

DALEK OPERATORS:

Robert Jewell – Lead Dalek Operator
Six others

VOICES:

Peter Hawkins
David Graham

SHAWCRAFT MODELS

Shawcraft Models had already been making props for the television series *Doctor Who* for several years when they were commissioned to make the feature film Daleks. The company was the brainchild of a trio of skilled men: Reg Haynes, a former army aircraft recognition instructor who also worked as a professional cartoonist; Stan Wilkins, former RAF engineer; and aircraft engineer Bill Roberts.

With their joint military backgrounds, their first jobs were for Woodason Aircraft Models. The men made detailed miniature aircraft for advertising and professional displays. Their first commission for the film industry was a replica Vickers Vimy for British Lion Films with a wingspan of sixty-seven feet. The men were experts in building with fibreglass, which made their work in high demand as few people had the expertise in this area. They would create models for many iconic films, such as their forty-foot model of the Titanic for *A Night to Remember* (1958).

For *Doctor Who*, in 1963, one of their first and most significant contributions was the TARDIS console, with its array of lights and rising central column. When making a practical version of BBC designer Raymond Cusick's Dalek sketches, they decided to base the scale around a man seated in an office chair on wheels. The feature film Daleks in 1965 were created from updated moulds of the original, with high skirting, longer bodies and brushed metal finishes. With more time and money, these were to be a significant upgrade on their television cousins. Shawcraft produced eight fully workable Dalek units for £2,400.

BELOW: The design team at Shawcraft Models gets to grips with the Daleks for the first film at their workshop. Photos from David J Howe.

REMEMBRANCE OF A DALEK

Bryan Hands was a young out-of-work actor when he got the call to join the first Dalek film. One of the operators had been taken ill during filming, and Bryan was found through the actor's directory Spotlight. "I wondered why they were asking me. Did I look like a Dalek? No, it was my height. They needed a performer who was under five foot seven to fit into the Dalek. They were desperate for someone to come along and take his place. So the next day, I was down at Shepperton, and I became a Dalek.". Gordon Flemyng knew strength would also be a key factor in the success of the Dalek operators. "What we needed was small but quite strong people. It was actually quite tiring to move those things around all day."

When he arrived at the studio, Hands was impressed with the Stage H sets. "They had the whole thing built in that studio so you could move around from one [set] to the other. You could see *Doctor Who*'s sitting room, the corridors built mainly of a sort of corrugated plastic sheeting. The crew from the sides operates the sliding doors. There was a vast area of woodland where the Thals were. Lastly, you could see the Dalek control centre, which was quite an elaborate set."

Hands got a crash course in Dalek movement from the other operators. "The technicians on the set showed what to do. It wasn't exactly rocket science. They lifted the lid, and you just climbed in and sat on the seat. You operated it with your feet on castors. You just sat in there and pushed and pulled it around, and they added controls for the hands. You could swivel the head with a lever and operate the arm, and the gun was a fire extinguisher. You pulled the trigger, and the steam shot out."

Hands got a chance to work inside several different Daleks. "They moved me around into red and blue Daleks, and I was even in the leader black Dalek too. Sometimes you were just stationary in the background, and maybe you just operated that arm, and then other times you were trundling along the corridors."

The excitement of the on-screen action is not matched by the slow pace of a film shoot. "You spend a lot of time sitting around waiting for something to happen. The Dalek operators would sit around in the corner playing cards until they were called and randomly selected for each machine." There was a script that Hands and his fellow actors had to follow. "Although none of our voices was used. We did learn the scene and the dialogue so we could come in at the right time pointing at the right person."

Hands fondly remembers his time on a well-paid job: £10 per day, the average weekly wage in the UK in 1965. Sadly he didn't return for the sequel. However, the performer he replaced was soon back on set, and as most came from the same agency it was simply more efficient to continue with the same troupe of actors.

BELOW: Actor Bryan Hands portrait head shot from 1965.

BELOW RIGHT: Robert Jewell inspects the Daleks' troops on *Invasion Earth*.

DALEK AUCTION

In 2020 The Prop Store auctioned this Dalek from *Invasion Earth*. The catalogue description says Shawcraft Models built this and, over the years, it has been modified and restored. Interestingly it does have its original wooden bench operator seat inside. Its lights are now blue jam jars. Accurate measurements confirm the size as 127 cm by 83 cm by 165 cm. Thanks to Prop Store for sharing previously unpublished images for this book.

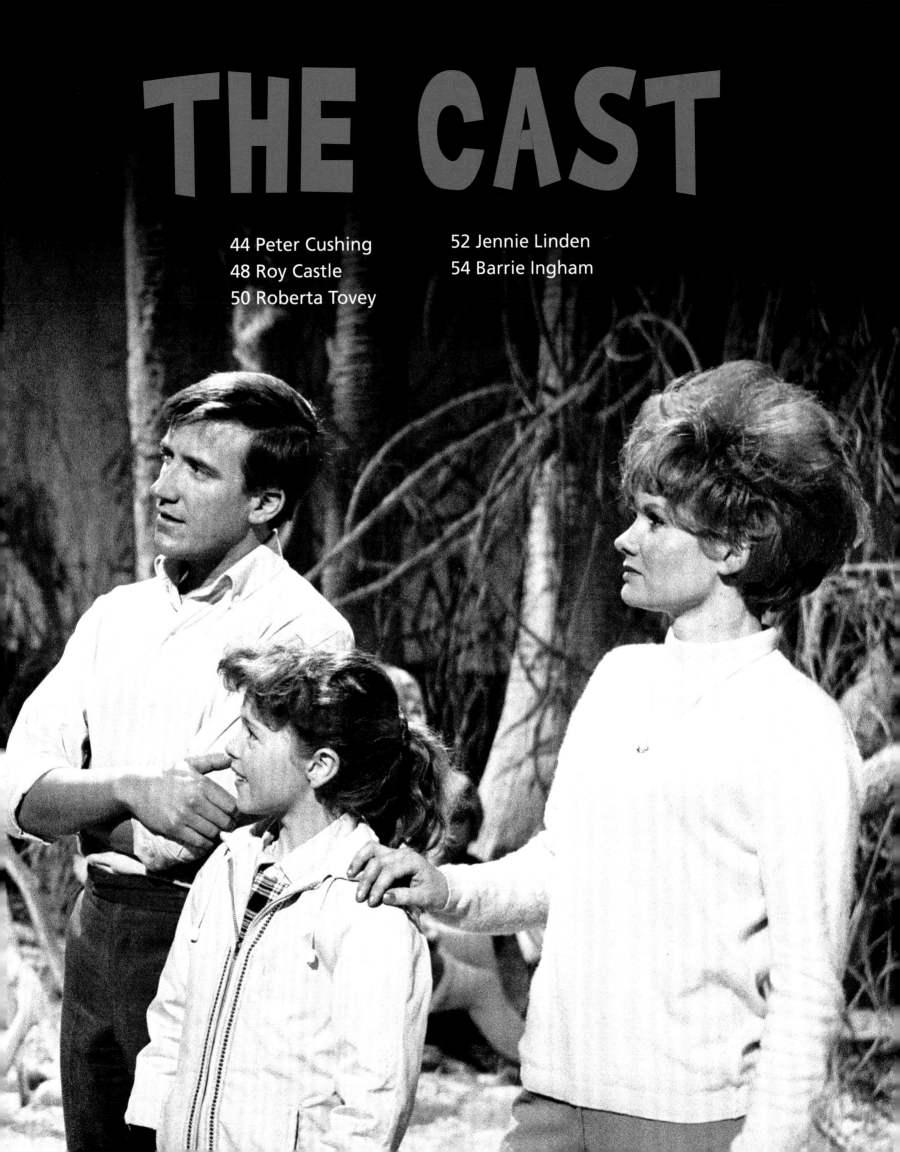

THE CAST

PETER CUSHING

By the time Peter Cushing was cast in the lead for *Dr. Who & The Daleks* in 1965, he was already an established film and television actor. His first film appearance was *The Man in the Iron Mask* (1939); however, audiences would have known him best for his successful parts in Hammer horror films. Despite some high-profile film roles, Cushing found it increasingly difficult to find parts in the post-war world. This changed after his starring role in the BBC adaptation of George Orwell's bleak science fiction novel *Nineteen Eighty-Four* (1954).

By the time he played Dr. Who, he had starred in over ten horror films. It would be his appearance in Amicus Film's successful anthology feature film, *Dr Terror's House of Horrors* (1965), that would cement his casting as the Time Lord. Outside of his horror appearances Cushing was best known as Grand Moff Wilhuff Tarkin in the original *Star Wars* (1977).

Cushing recalled the plan for the films was to set a somewhat darker, more serious tone than what was eventually delivered. "We intended to make them a little darker."

When the question came up about the differences between his own on-screen portrayal of the first Doctor and that of William Hartnell, Cushing had devised a very clever answer worthy of the Time Lord himself. Cushing was a fan of the series but didn't watch it religiously due to the pressures of work at the time. "One of the few episodes of the *Doctor Who* series that I saw involved a kind of mystical clown ('The Celestial Toymaker'), and I realised that perhaps he kidnapped Doctor Who and wiped his memory and made him relive some of his earlier adventures. When Bill Hartnell turned into Patrick Troughton and changed his appearance, that idea seemed more likely. I think that's what happened, so I think those films we did fit perfectly well into the TV series. That would not have been the case had I taken the role in the TV series."

Cushing was meticulous in both his on-screen and off-screen personas. Between takes, Peter Cushing would wear white cotton gloves supplied by the editing department. He was a smoker and was keen not to get any nicotine stains on his fingers. All of

those who worked with Cushing were positive about his work and attitude. He did have a costume requirement on all his films: he requested a blue silk scarf, necktie or cravat to bring out his piercing blue eyes. He would ask to keep the clothes from his many Victorian films.

Cushing was himself asked about taking on the role of the Doctor on television after his successful big-screen outings. "When Bill Hartnell was forced to quit, I was asked if I would be interested in taking the lead in the new series. I turned it down, which I now regret a little. It would have been fun. But at the time, you know, I considered myself a serious film actor, and stepping into a television series seemed like a step backwards. I don't know how serious the producers were about hiring me. But perhaps if I'd said yes, they would have been pleased, and you would have had me fighting Daleks and Cybermen week in, week out. But I'm glad I didn't in some ways because Patrick was so wonderful."

Producers asked again when looking to cast a role during the Tom Baker era. "I don't know the part, but they wanted me, and I was interested, but scheduling conflicts scuppered it. But perhaps in the future, I'll be able to take part. I'd be very keen on that."

Cushing's final film role would be another time travel adventure, the British feature film *Biggles* (1996).

ROY CASTLE

Before his casting in *Dr. Who & The Daleks*, Roy Castle was known as a comedian, dancer and entertainer more than a straight actor. As Ian, he played the love interest to Dr. Who's older granddaughter, Barbara, played by Jennie Linden. However, he was best known on British television for his BBC children's series *Record Breakers*, which ran for twenty years.

Being at the heart of the BBC and in the homes of millions of viewers each week, Castle was regularly identified as being a former *Doctor Who* companion. He remembered and enjoyed his time in the film and recognised its legacy with fans. "It was quite unusual. Very unlike anything I've ever done, but I still get letters about it even today, requests for me to sign things and pop them back in the mail. Crazy, far more than I get for anything else. Sometimes they come up to me in the street. I had a very small part to play in something that's become this very big, well quite big, television institution."

Castle believes the indelible image of the big screen Daleks helped cement the series' longevity. "We kicked it all off. I never imagined I'd still be asked about it twenty years later."

Despite sharing the screen with one of the biggest stars in British cinema, Castle felt he and Peter Cushing were upstaged by the shiny new Daleks that cost thousands to create for the film. "The Daleks were brilliant. I think if you'd said to the producer, you must get rid of the humans or the Daleks, he'd have got rid of us humans in a flash. He knew they were his money ticket. I remember that much. I think he was a little bit in love with them. You had Peter Cushing, this very respectable and successful British actor, and the producer barely spoke to him, too busy polishing his Daleks. Metaphorically, that is."

Roberta Tovey played twelve-year-old Susie and recalls Castle's melodic contribution to the shoot.

"Some days, he would bring his trumpet to the studios with him to practice things. But the trouble was, he had the dressing room down the corridor to me. When I wasn't on set, I used to have to be doing my schoolwork. Roy would start playing all these songs. And then you'd get carried away and sort of start singing along with the some of the tunes that you recognized he was playing. In the end I'd give up and send a message down to him and say, "Well, can you play this one?""

Roy Castle and Peter Cushing would die within a month of each other in 1994, both of cancer. Cushing was 81 and Castle was 62.

ROBERTA TOVEY

The youngest member of the cast at age 12, Roberta Tovey played Dr. Who's granddaughter Susan, or "Susie", as she was called on screen. Her television counterpart was played by Carole Ann Ford, who was 25 in 1965, but screenwriter and producer Milton Subotsky hoped to include all audience members by having a child in a central role. Tovey was a fan of the series and was thrilled to be cast. "I had watched the TV series with William Hartnell playing Doctor Who. So I knew what it was about and the thought of actually doing it on film… I was thrilled."

Tovey also recognised that rewriting the leading characters would help bring a larger audience to the film version. "From the series, Ian and Barbara were like two school teachers. But with our film, it was Dr. Who, Susan and Barbara were his granddaughters, and Ian was the love interest. I think it made it more family-oriented with a much warmer atmosphere."

Peter Cushing's portrayal of the older Doctor character made a vivid impression on Tovey, so much so that she failed to recognise him outside of the character make up. "Peter was much younger than the part he was portraying. When I came on set Peter would already be there dressed as Dr. Who and have a wig and bushy eyebrows. I had to do a scene where I put one of the Thals' capes under a Dalek to stop it working. They called Peter down to do an eyeline shot off camera. He had been cleared for filming for the day. So he'd obviously removed his wig and bushy eyebrows and was in his own clothes before going home. I got quite a shock from that because I'd only seen him with his white hair before and he looked quite different."

The realistic landscape of the Dalek planet Skaro impressed the young Tovey, who had seen the modest BBC Television version in 1963. The vast Shepperton Studios sound stage held the petrified forest set and the metallic Dalek city interiors. "It was quite magical. And for a time, you believed you were on another planet. And they built the Dalek city far to the other end of the studio. And we could actually look as though we saw the Dalek city in the distance – it was all there for us."

Tovey would return to the sequel on the insistence of star Peter Cushing. Despite her age Tovey fitted well into the cast and even got the nickname "one-take Tovey". Director Gordon Flemyng offered the young actress a shilling for each take she got in the first attempt. She was presented with a purse full of shillings at the end of the production.

JENNIE LINDEN

Jennie Linden would play Barbara, the granddaughter of Dr. Who. In the 1963 television version series the role of Barbara Wright was played by Jacqueline Hill. The role was that of a history teacher at Coal Hill School in London. For the feature film version Milton Subotsky wanted to make it a more close-knit family, and Barbara was made his elder granddaughter.

Jennie Linden had caught the eye of producers after appearing in the Hammer Horror film *Nightmare* (1964) directed by Freddie Francis. Francis had worked with Milton Subotsky's Amicus Films and was first choice to take the helm for the first big screen *Dr. Who & The Daleks* film.

Linden would not return for the sequel as she was pursuing major films and had a screen test for *The Lion in Winter* (1966), with Peter O'Toole. She was unsuccessful but was also anxious about being typecast in what she saw as a children's film.

"And I did feel a little nervous in doing two films, because on the *Doctor Who* theme, I realized how popular and cultish *Doctor Who* was becoming and I didn't really want to be associated with one particular storyline. I wasn't available for [the sequel] because I was too busy trying to move in another direction. It doesn't mean I didn't enjoy it I did and it was lovely. Great fun to do. I wouldn't have missed it for the world."

Linden would go on to success with her BAFTA-nominated role in Ken Russell's *Women in Love* (1969).

BARRIE INGHAM

BELOW LEFT:
Michael Coles as
Ganatus alongside Thal
co-star, fashion model
Jane Lumb.

BELOW RIGHT:
Peter Cushing and
Barrie Ingham on the
Skaro forest set.

Barrie Ingham's role as Alydon was the principal alien speaking part in the film other than the Daleks. This would only be Ingham's second film role, but he had considerably more acting experience than many of his fellow alien co-stars. Most of the Thals on the planet Skaro were cast for their impressive physical presence, as Ingham recalls. "They got the real Covent Garden porters. They got the guys who sling the apples and pears. And they were tough guys, until the moment when they got into makeup and started putting eyebrows on like Jean Shrimpton."

The alien transformation of the burly six-foot-plus men didn't stop at the face. Each had to shave their arms and chest hair. "They couldn't believe it because this was absolutely a blow against their masculinity. It was like Samson and Delilah." They were all compensated with an extra pound a day. "It changed the personalities; they all became a little bit more subdued and things. The moral of that story is every Thal has his price."

Ingham was impressed by the production and thought he had his first-day film nerves under control. "My first shot was with Peter Cushing. It was his first scene in the film, too, when we're both sitting by the fireside. Just before the take, this vastly experienced film actor said, "Oh, gosh, I feel so nervous, don't

you, before the first scene in the film?", and because he asked me, I had forgotten my nerves. We had a lovely scene and never had any nerves. That's the kind of guy he was. He did it quite deliberately to put me at my ease."

In the same year the film was released, Ingham appeared in the television series *Doctor Who* playing the character of Paris in 'The Myth Makers'. The four-part adventure was set in ancient Troy and based on the *Iliad* by Homer, in which the Greek army besieges the walled city of Troy for ten years. All four episodes are missing, believed wiped; from 1967 to 1978, the BBC would wipe videotape masters of *Doctor Who* and other programmes for storage reasons, and in some instances to reuse the costly videotapes.

In reality the tapes were rarely reused, and sometimes the strict Equity rules on actors' repeat fees and contracts would be claimed as a reason to put some episodes beyond use. A lack of clear policy meant thousands of tapes were erased and later dumped when programme producers did not reuse them. It was a perfect storm of factors leading to the loss of many episodes of the programme in the 1960s and well into the 1970s; almost a hundred are missing and likely to have been lost entirely.

DR. WHO & THE DALEKS (1965)

The Story

TARDIS is the latest invention of Dr. Who (PETER CUSHING). A Time And Relative Dimension In Space machine, it can transport passengers to another world, at another time.

With his granddaughters Barbara (JENNIE LINDEN) and Susan (ROBERTA TOVEY), Dr. Who demonstrates the machine to Barbara's boy-friend, Ian (ROY CASTLE). Ian trips and stumbles against the control panel. And the four humans are instantly ejected away from Earth.

The arrival

Landing in a vast petrified forest, they find a box of drugs mysteriously placed near their spaceship. Leaving these inside TARDIS, they set out to explore a futuristic city, glistening beyond the forest on the horizon.

This, they discover, is the all-metal city of Daleks. A greedy warmongering form of life, the Daleks are shielded by mobile metal cones and armed with flame guns which can temporarily cripple. The cones and city protect the Daleks from radiation, which has ravaged their planet since a massive neutron war.

Captured

Dr. Who and his party are taken prisoner. And Susan, the youngest and least affected by the polluted atmosphere, is sent to collect the drugs—assumed to counteract radiation—

from inside TARDIS. The Daleks' aim is to copy the drugs, emerge from their protective city and ultimately to destroy the only other form of life on the planet . . . the Thals.

On her way Susan meets Alydon (BARRIE INGHAM). Gentle and friendly, he is leader of the Thals. It was he who had left the drugs for the visitors from Earth. He now gives Susan his white plastic cape and asks her to carry a message of friendship to the Daleks, together with a request for food for his starving people.

Death of a Dalek

Back at the metal city, the Daleks trick Susan into inviting the Thals to collect food. But Dr. Who deduces that the Daleks are generated by power from the metal floors. Covering their cell with Alydon's plastic cape, the humans capture their jailer. Cut off from the generating power, the gruesome creature dies. . . .

Meanwhile, an array of Daleks lie in ambush for the approaching Thals. The escaped prisoners shout a warning just in time. And, as the Daleks open fire, most of the Thals escape from the city with the visitors from Earth.

The Dalek bomb

Discovering that they cannot be protected by the drug, the Daleks decide to explode a

giant neutron bomb. This will increase radiation and exterminate the Thals.

Flashing mirrors to confuse the guards, Dr. Who, Alydon and a party of Thals attack Dalek City. The trick fails. Dr. Who is taken prisoner. But Alydon escapes to round up a relief army of Thals.

Crossing massive chasms and monster-infested swamps, Ian, Barbara and two Thals enter the city through an unguarded front. In a corridor they are cornered by two Daleks who open fire. Alydon and his relief army arrive just in time. They up-end the Daleks who are immediately destroyed by their own flames.

Count down

In the control room, a count down has already started on the neutron bomb. Daleks and Thals fight out a terrible battle. Ian helplessly tries to switch off the mechanism. The Daleks fire on him furiously. He ducks. And the whole panel goes up in flames.

Daleks destroyed

With the count down arrested and power cut off, the Daleks are exterminated. The Thals are free to live in peace on their far-away planet. And Dr. Who and his party can return to TARDIS and—they hope—Earth. . . .

The Cast

Dr. Who	PETER CUSHING	Temmosus	GEOFFREY TOONE
Ian	ROY CASTLE	Elyon	MARK PETERSEN
Barbara	JENNIE LINDEN	Antodus	JOHN BOWN
Susan	ROBERTA TOVEY	Ganatus	MICHAEL COLES
Alydon	BARRIE INGHAM	Dyoni	YVONNE ANTROBUS

Technical Credits

Executive Producer	JOE VEGODA	Art Director	BILL CONSTABLE	Make-up	JILL CARPENTER
Producers	MILTON SUBOTSKY and MAX J. ROSENBERG	Editor	OSWALD HAFENRICHTER	Hairdresser	HENRY MONTSASH
		Camera Operator	DAVID HARCOURT	Wardrobe Mistress	JACKIE CUMMINS
Director	GORDON FLEMYNG	Assistant Director	ANTHONY WAYE	Stills Cameraman	TED REED
Production Manager	TED LLOYD	Sound Mixer	BUSTER AMBLER	Asst. Art Director	KEN RYAN
Lighting Cameraman	JOHN WILCOX	Continuity	PAMELA DAVIES	Set Dresser	SCOTT SLIMON

Length 7436 ft.   **Certificate "U"**   **Running Time** 83 mins.   **Reg. No.** BR/E 30512

THE SHOOT

BELOW: Roy Castle's character Ian is as petrified as the beast he meets – which was made out of plaster.

OPPOSITE: The original press release for the film.

In February 1965 Joe Vegoda submitted the script to the British Board of Film Censors to try and get ahead of any cuts that might later have to be made. This was common practice at the time; Ray Harryhausen's *Jason and the Argonauts* (1963) was submitted, then titled *Jason and the Golden Fleece*, and the iconic skeleton fight sequence had to be changed significantly. For *Dr. Who & The Daleks* changes would include the removal of screaming from the main characters, and of extreme peril such as close-ups of the reptile creature. Milton Subotsky would have been happy to go along with the changes as he knew that a "U" certificate was vital for the producers, who didn't want anyone refused entry to their film.

Principal photography commenced on Friday 12th March 1965 for the six-week shoot. The budget was £180,000, higher than any film that Milton Subotsky had produced before.

It would be a challenge to make a truly lavish science-fiction spectacle on that money, but Subotsky knew that securing the largest sound stage in Europe would be the starting point. Shepperton's legendary Stage H had been home to *Mysterious Island* (1961), *Lawrence of Arabia* (1962) and *Dr Strangelove* (1964). After *Dr. Who*, other prestigious cinematic sci-fi guests would include *2001: A Space Odyssey* (1968), *The Omen* (1976), *Star Wars* (1977), *Superman* (1978), *Alien* (1979) and *Flash Gordon* (1980). Anthony Waye was the First Assistant Director and worked closely with Director Gordon Flemyng. He told me that Subotsky was canny with the deal for the studio hire. "Subotsky made quite a few small films at Shepperton so as we shot in February/March when the industry was quiet, he probably got a good deal."

There would be no location work on this first Dalek film. Instead, the controlled and costly environment of the sound stage would become home to the production for the next six weeks. Contracts were turned around fast, and within two weeks of signing, the main cast was on set and filming their first scenes.

The stars of the film were, of course, the Daleks. Their scenes were shot in two blocks in April 1965. BBC Dalek operators came to train the others: Robert Jewell, Kevin Man and Gerald Taylor created the choreography for the other Daleks to move and act consistently and, most importantly, not to bump into the expensive sets. Once filming was complete, the men returned to the BBC to film the *Doctor Who* serial 'The Chase', which featured the Daleks alongside a new metal menace, the Mechanoids.

The Daleks' voices should have been in sync with their head-top lights at both sides of their domes, but it was only noticed a week into the shoot that these had been flashing randomly. Subotsky had to rewrite their dialogue in the editing room to match with the flashes from the lights.

The scenes of the petrified forest of war-torn Skaro (although the planet is never referred to by name in the first film) and the vast Dalek city would be best accommodated in Europe's biggest soundstage, Stage H. 45 feet high and with 30,000 square feet of floor space, Stage H would be the main setting for the production. It also had an interior tank, which measured 25 feet by 12 feet

by 3 feet. This was used for underwater filming on *Mysterious Island* (1960) and in *Flash Gordon* (1980) as the Arborian swamp prison. It would be best remembered for a dry shoot when the tank was expanded to create a sunken area measuring 60 feet by 120 feet by 60 feet – the cavernous moon surface where the monolith is found in Stanley Kubrick's *2001 A Space Odyssey* (1968).

The Dalek City set would take up 18,000 square feet of Stage H at the cost of £13,000. "It's probably the world's first plastic set", declared Subotsky. "It's all plastic, but it looks metallic. We used all sorts of new materials." The scale of the production came as a surprise to Jennie Linden. "We were shown the main set by Milton Subotsky, and I remember being incredibly impressed because it was so big. It was then that I thought, oh, this is a major film. It was the famous Stage H at Shepperton, and it was suddenly ours, and it built this entire landscape."

There would be a change to the TARDIS, too, as the film's producers did not agree to use the iconic central console design.

ABOVE: The framing of the Daleks makes full use of the widescreen format.

BELOW: This now-iconic image formed part of Tom Chantrell's poster art.

Instead, the big-screen time machine resembled the messy inside of a large radio set. Linden recalls being intimidated on her first day. "The TARDIS was so complex, and when you come on to do a scene, you're coming on in quite a nervous state. It was not that small. It had various corners and parts of it with all these wires hanging down. You would be doing a scene in a certain part of that semi-circular set. To get the cameras in the first shot of the film, it was an enclosed room. Then they opened up the set, as they do, to get the cameras in."

Co-star Roberta Tovey, who played 12-year-old Susie, was surprised by the design of the TARDIS. "It threw me when I first saw it because I was expecting the television series version, with the round console in the middle. This was all wires and things everywhere. I don't know whether I was disappointed or it just threw me because it was so different." The Daleks, too, were a surprise for the youngster. "I noticed that they were bigger when I first saw them. And very colourful and taller." For Linden, it was a surprise that they had operators inside. "I had a shock where I didn't realise for ages who was inside the Daleks. I got very busy on lines and plot and where I should be. I didn't often see my surroundings in a very observant way. It was later on that I realised that there was a very small guy in there operating them."

The forest set made a big impact on Tovey when she saw it for the first time, though she was cautious about its delicate

DR. WHO & THE DALEKS: THE OFFICIAL STORY OF THE FILMS

nature. "The set was always quite dark and I remember you had to be very careful about touching everything because everything was made of fibreglass. So you really had to be careful where you were walking, and of all the sand. It was quite magical. It was quite enchanting. Sort of an *Alice in Wonderland*."

The first days of shooting were the opening scenes of the film. But as the days progressed, the order of the scenes filmed was dictated by the available sets and the number of actors needed for each scene. It would be costly to have extras sat around waiting to be called. The standing sets were required to be used to their maximum before they were taken down and replaced. Overrunning would cost the tightly budgeted production thousands, so long hours were the norm for the duration of the shoot. This was only Linden's second film and remembering where her character was challenging at times. "As we began to shoot out of [scene] order with a lot of running through doors and down corridors, things would be a bit similar to others. That's where we all, including Peter, got caught out a bit as to where we were in the acting."

The shoot wrapped on 23rd April 1965. None of the production team or cast could have imagined the film's staying power. Tovey says she didn't have any idea of the legacy the film would have. "I don't think we appreciated at the time how big it would become. I know I certainly didn't. Many 1960s films are very dated. This always seems to stand the test of time. It's timeless." Even today, Linden gets asked more about this film than any of her many other roles. "All the memorabilia clubs and seminars I've attended, it is unbelievable how keen the fans are. They can't hear you talk about it enough and explain everything. I didn't know that it would be such a cult. I look back on my 40-year career and think it was the only thing I've ever done. It is only *Doctor Who* letters I seem to get now."

ART DIRECTOR

OPPOSITE: Dr. Who, Ian, Barbara and Susan get their first glimpse of Skaro. Colourisation by Clayton Hickman.

The responsibility for creating a new Dalek City, the TARDIS and the surface of the planet Skaro fell to Australian Bill Constable. Constable is best known for his theatre work, designing over 160 dramas, operas and ballets including costumes and sets for *London Morning*, Noël Coward's only ballet. His first significant film work was as Art Director on the feature film *Long John Silver* (1954).

By the 1960s, Constable was predominantly an Art Director for feature films. Today he would be called a Production Designer. For the newly formed Amicus Films, he designed the teenage musical *Just for Fun* (1963), directed by Gordon Flemyng. Next was *Dr Terror's House of Horrors* (1964) with Peter Cushing and Roy Castle. Freddie Francis directed, the original director asked to shoot *Dr. Who*'s motion picture debut. Constable would go on to work on ten more Amicus films.

When Freddie Francis turned down the offer of the Dalek film, Gordon Flemyng took the director's chair. Constable and Flemyng had become good friends, so when the opportunity presented itself for Constable's daughter Dee to audition for the part of 12-year-old Susan, she jumped at the chance.

Dee told me about the audition, which was filmed at Shepperton Studios. "It was a really good experience. But I think that was more about who my dad was than anything about me." Dee recalls how friendly both Gordon Flemyng and Milton Subotsky were. "I remember Milton used to give me Christmas presents. He was very sweet." In their Holland Park flat in London, Dee remembers being surrounded by her father's art and painting. It was here that Dee saw production designs

and technical drawings for both theatre and film. "It didn't seem unusual to me as that was Dad's way of working but looking back, this was a wonderfully creative and artistic time."

The visuals on a production like this would make or break a science fiction film. Subotsky explained this to *Kinematograph Weekly* in March 1965: "We intend to make full use of the colour, spectacle and action that marks the difference between large and small screen entertainment." Indeed, Constable's artistic contribution to *Dr. Who & The Daleks* has given the film a high production value compared to its relatively modest budget, and his design aesthetic endures today.

PLANET SKARO

Only two of Constable's artworks are known to survive – a landscape image of the mountainous Skaro surface and a piece of concept art for the TARDIS interior. Constable's Skaro landscape would have been the basis for Gerald Larn's matte painting used in the final sequence. "There would have been several paintings created for each set and from different angles. There would be smaller storyboards too." Dee recalls her father being hands-on with the construction too. "I remember him

working closely with the set builders and the set dressers." This is the only artwork from the *Dr. Who* movie still in the Constable family collection.

Milton Subotsky was keen to champion his films and the behind-the-scenes talent. He told *Doctor Who Bulletin* in September 1990 that they worked with Bill Constable as often as possible. "He was very good and we worked very well with him. The petrified forest was very good. I thought that design was excellent, as was the hill going up to the city which opened up and which everyone fell in. We tried as far as possible, within the confines of the budget, to give people a big picture."

Skaro's forest of petrified trees was made from plaster of Paris and hung upside down to create the otherworldly effect. There is an effective theatrical painted backdrop that extends the trees and foliage of the set; Constable's theatre work would have made him ideally positioned to get the best from this technique. John Wilcox's green, almost comic-book-style lighting of these scenes lends to the otherworldly atmosphere and gives the forest a sense of depth that could not have been achieved in black and white. Fifteen years later Stage H at Shepperton would be home to an almost identical forest for the planet Arboria in *Flash Gordon* (1980).

ABOVE: Artwork here courtesy of the Constable family which owns the original cliffside painting, which measures 34 cm by 70 cm.

NEW TARDIS

The TARDIS set was a controversial move away from in-house BBC designer Peter Brachacki's streamlined console with the rising centre column. Subotsky supported his Art Director's choice. "Bill Constable decided to design his own and I accepted his design. We wanted something that was very spacious inside. In fact, if you look at the TARDIS on television over the years, it has changed quite a bit. We just wanted to do our own thing."

The artwork seen here closely represents the on-screen creation for the film, combining elements of a big transistor radio and a practical science laboratory. This piece measures 33 centimetres by 64 centimetres. Dee reveals her father's working practice: "Bill would not measure by eye but preferred to take a piece of paper and draw an internal frame using his set square, as he always had in mind the practical nature of the set needing to be built." Some of Constable's visual flourishes would endure: the interior TARDIS white police box doors would appear in the relaunched *Doctor Who* television series in 2005; and by the time Matt Smith became the Doctor in 2010 the TARDIS exterior entrance door would once again be emblazoned with the star logo of St John's Ambulance.

Director Flemyng liked the new design for the time machine. "Because the film was being made for the wide screen, we wanted to make everything bigger and better. We wanted you to feel that when you went into the TARDIS, it was huge. It was supposed to have been cobbled together by the Doctor in his back garden and we made the wires and lights multi-coloured so it would all seem bolder than the TV version."

OPPOSITE: The original TARDIS interior production painting by Bill Constable, and the final film version below. Courtesy of Davidson Auctions.

RIGHT: The TARDIS exterior. Colourisation by Clayton Hickman.

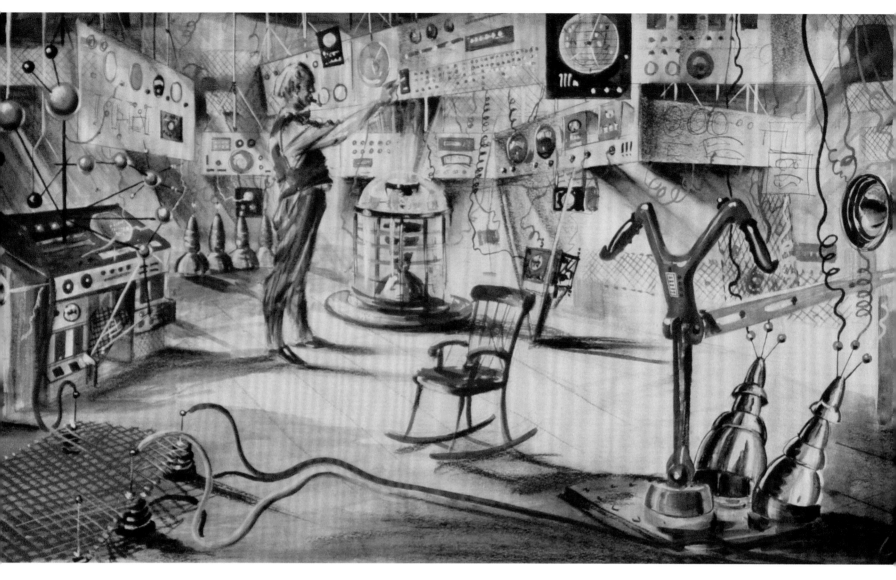

DR. WHO & THE DALEKS : THE OFFICIAL STORY OF THE FILMS

PLASTIC FANTASTIC

Constable's acclaimed theatre work gave him a new viewpoint when it came to designing for film. Dee recalls his practical theatrical techniques being carried across to his film work and *Dr. Who.* "He used to use the model theatre to get the perspective correct. Which is different in the film than theatre, but he had such an understanding of that discipline".

Subotsky was keen for the audience to appreciate the lavish scale of this first big-screen outing of Dr. Who and those often-unsung heroes behind the scenes. He told *Kinematography Weekly* in 1965, "Our real star of the film is Bill Constable, who designed the sets. It's probably the world's first plastic set. It's all in plastic, but it looks metallic. We've used all sorts of new materials." These new materials included transparent coloured Perspex, which allowed for clever use of pulse lighting from Director of Photography John Wilcox. The film's finale set would not be out of place in a James Bond adventure; the Dalek control room was estimated to have cost £3,000.

Flemyng appreciated the practical design elements of the Dalek city interior. "The doors in their city opened from the centre and were wide at the bottom, narrow at the top. Dalek-shaped. The city was designed by Daleks for Daleks."

Constable did not design the sequel but did continue working with producer Subotsky. Dee believes it was simply the pressure of work that meant he didn't work on *Daleks' Invasion Earth 2150 A.D.* the following year, and his interests did not just lie in science fiction or horror. "The variety of something new would have appealed to him." In his lifetime Dee believes her father didn't get the credit he deserved. "Bill's work was under-appreciated at the time, and today the Australian National Library, National Gallery and the Gallery of New South Wales all have collections of my father's work. When you see his work *en masse*, you can see his eye and his flair for design." Dee is hopeful that more of her father's work on the film might resurface. "It would be fascinating and exciting to see anything that is newly discovered."

ABOVE: The full colour Dalek City design distanced the film from the television series.

BELOW: An epic scale of production design more akin to a James Bond film.

DIRECTOR'S CHAIR: GORDON FLEMYNG

BELOW: Gordon Flemyng during a shoot for *The Avengers* (1967).

OPPOSITE: First Assistant Director Anthony Waye and Gordon Flemyng on the Dalek saucer set for *Invasion Earth*.

Keen to replicate the success in front of and behind the camera of *Dr Terror's House of Horrors* (1965), Subotsky would offer Freddie Francis the Director's chair for *Dr. Who & The Daleks*. In his memoir, Francis recalls turning it down. "Although it was an enormous success, as was the sequel, I have never regretted my decision not to direct it. When I read the script, I realised that the budget just wouldn't cover what was required. I wrote a letter to Milton explaining my reasons and pointing out that the script called for hundreds of Daleks and the budget would only cover a handful at most."

Gordon Flemyng took on the assignment – and the task of creating legions of Daleks on screen. He had directed three feature films,

including the 1963 musical *Just for Fun* for Milton Subotsky's Amicus Productions. Flemyng was also an accomplished camera operator, and as *Dr. Who & The Daleks* had a tight budget and an ambitious technical script, he was the right director for the job. His son is the screen actor Jason Flemyng, and although he was only one year old in 1965, he cites his father as the prime motivator in his career. "Gordon Flemyng was probably my biggest inspiration for getting into the business. I have spent the last twenty years collecting anything I can get that's got footage of him – it is important to me."

Subotsky was keen to give new opportunities to actors and directors but was sometimes dismissive of what they could bring to one of his films. He told *Starburst Magazine* that "The script

OPPOSITE ABOVE:
Gordon Flemyng
discussing the scene
with the cast in the
Dalek City set.

ABOVE: Anthony
Waye, left, and Gordon
Flemyng on the
Destroyed London set
for *Invasion Earth*.

is the most important thing in film-making, and the editing. The direction is not that important. I think the cult of the director came into being because the critics have to attach some name to a film, and so they think the director is the man who makes the film, but he's not. I don't think it's all that important who directs a picture. That's one of the reasons we've given so many people their first picture to direct."

In *Kinematograph Weekly* in 1966, Flemyng commented on the reduced role and influence of the director in television and his love of cinema. "There's no longer any control for the director in TV. It's all with the producers now. Once the director did have the control: he got the script and he got the cast. But because almost all drama in TV now is series, control lies with the producer and he has the continuity. It has to be that way with that type of show. That's why TV people go into films, because the director has much more control."

Anthony Waye was the First Assistant Director and worked closely with Flemyng. Waye would have a thirty-year association with the James Bond film series as a senior production executive. He told me about his close working relationship with Flemyng. "I had worked on a film titled *The Skull* made by Amicus, which was also a Milton Subotsky

company. I also had worked with the Production Manager, we got on well. My salary was £60 per five-day week! Gordon, I got on with extremely well. I did not only have the two Dalek films with him, but I also did another big film in Hong Kong and Spain."

Jason Flemyng says that his dad was a "fiery character", but in the pressure-cooker environment of a modestly-budgeted film in the largest and most expensive sound stage in Europe, that is understandable. "He was famously good at what he did, famously loved by the people who were good at what they did, and hated by the people who weren't good." Flemyng would take over shots from camera operators if he felt he wasn't getting what he needed. Waye confirmed this to me. "Gordon could be fiery but as a First A.D. you were used to dealing with grumpy producers, directors, actors and sometimes crew members. I either ignored him, shouted back or sorted out the problem that was causing him grief." Waye recalls Flemyng as a creative collaborator: "Gordon could plan a shot list and we could add to it with suggestions."

Despite the sizeable creative shadow that producer Milton Subotsky cast on the film, Jennie Linden recalls that he was rarely seen on set by the cast. "I saw him once or twice. I

remember Peter chatting to him quite a bit. But I didn't find him that approachable. Joe Vegoda was more visible, but a lot was left to Gordon." Tovey agrees. "My memory is of Gordon being in charge of everything." Flemyng and Waye together kept the production on schedule and budget, acting as much as producers as anyone else on set. Waye recalls, "He was meticulous in his work, and you can see it in the films with his continuity. He was charming to us on the set. He was always even-tempered." Waye worked closely with the director to keep on schedule. "I would have done the shooting schedule from

that script. I certainly went to daily rushes but would have left the film on completion so didn't get involved in editing."

The youngest cast member, 12-year-old Roberta Tovey, remembers Flemyng fondly. "I had to climb down [a slope]. And I think Gordon Flemyng at the time saw the look of horror on my face. It was quite slippery and made of fibreglass. The camera was to stand at the top and pan down with me. I think he saw me looking over the edge, and he said, "Don't worry, I'll come down with you. I'll just be behind the camera, and I'll catch you if you fall." So I put my faith in him and said okay, all right. I'll do it."

ABOVE: A 12-year-old Roberta Tovey becomes the youngest stunt performer of the shoot – and more was to come for the sequel.

DR WHO & THE DALEKS: THE OFFICIAL STORY OF THE FILMS

The fiery side of the Glaswegian director was not far from the surface, as Jennie Linden would discover. Shepperton Studios had a hotel next door with a large bar that served drinks into the small hours. Along with her fellow young Thal cast members, Linden would sometimes drink through the night and return to work the following day from the pub without going to bed. "So there you are the next morning at six o'clock in the makeup caravan. You haven't slept a wink. Gordon Flemyng got wind of this. He told us off for not following the script, not taking it seriously, and not paying attention. We were the naughty children of the class that day because Gordon was quite cross with us, to say the least."

Jason Flemyng admits to being scared of the big screen Daleks but loving that his dad was giving the orders. "They always terrified me, the Daleks, and watching Dad's film now it's funny because there is still a fear factor to them. It's hard for

me to divorce myself from the image because my dad is six feet away from every shot taken in that film. And that's something which bonds me to those films."

From the more than one hundred films he had been involved in, Waye is surprised by which ones resurface for re-evaluation. "I'm constantly amazed at requests I get from way past films. The Daleks interest seems to be ongoing – I suppose recent TV series have helped keep it alive. They were certainly modestly-budgeted as were all Subotsky productions."

Flemyng was pragmatic about the metal stars of his films and their limitations. "They couldn't go upstairs and they couldn't go on anything that wasn't smooth." During a viewing of the footage known as rushes in the UK and dailies in the US, Flemyng accidentally came across a technique that would allow him to create an otherworldly effect in the forest scenes.

"I had gone into the viewing room to see the rushes from the previous day, but the person who had been in before me had been viewing his material through an anamorphic lens. They had forgotten to take the anamorphic lens out of the projector and all my rushes had this strange, unearthly quality, with all the angles not quite right and the pictures looking wrong somehow. I decided that we could use this effect in the film, so all the scenes in which we wanted the forest to look strange and alien, we filmed without the anamorphic lens on the camera, while the rest were filmed with the lens on. The distortion achieved was enough to give the film the alien look I was after."

ABOVE AND OPPOSITE: John Wilcox's lighting, with its strong primary colours, brings an otherworldly quality to the film.

RIGHT: Director of Photography John Wilcox with Gordon Flemyng on the multi-level Dalek Saucer set for *Invasion Earth*. Photo from Marcus Brooks / The UK Peter Cushing Appreciation Society.

MATTE PAINTINGS

BELOW: The first of two Gerald Larn paintings of the Skaro mountainside, this one from a distance.

BELOW RIGHT: The film set portion of the mountain with actors in shot.

The artistry of the matte painter often goes unnoticed. For example, if the script requires an extension to a domestic street, or a house on a hilltop, the matte painter can create this on a sheet of glass. The image is then filmed, often on location, to add extra scenery, set or backdrop as required. The only limitation is the imagination of the scriptwriters.

Gerald Larn started working at Shepperton Studios in 1965. He spent three years at Farnham School of Art, specialising in Painting. Not long after leaving, his work was being exhibited in London galleries. He got a job at Shepperton filling in for an absent matte artist and stayed for ten years.

Larn created the matte paintings on both Dalek films.

This first film had three paintings. Larn created two based on the Bill Constable concept art. These offered a close view of Barbara, Ian and the two Thals as they started their ascent of a mountain on planet Skaro. Alongside the screen images of the final composite, recently discovered photography being shown here for the first time depicts the live-action studio element on the foot of the mountain and the summit. Larn's matte paintings accompanied both viewpoints and would expand the landscape beyond anything that any film budget could accommodate in any other way.

OPPOSITE BELOW:
A closer view of the mountain vista with the cast now in place, climbing the rock face in the final composite.

ABOVE: The cast standing on a full size partial set of the Dalek City exterior.

BELOW: The Dalek City model as it appeared on set.

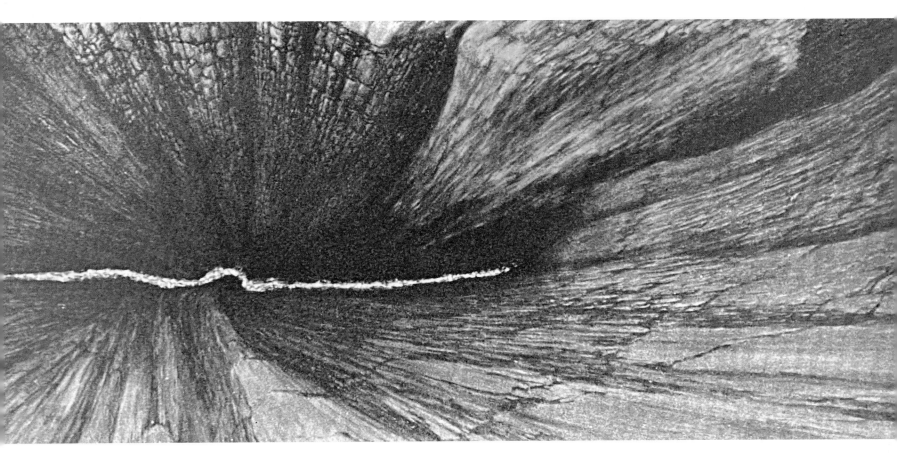

Larn's other matte painting would be the gorge. In a rare interview with visual effects historian Domingo Lizcano, Larn discusses this brief but effective shot. "You can also see the glistening river effect at the bottom of the gorge painting. We filmed some mirror-reflected light that was then burnt on at a low exposure to try and give some life to the shot."

Each artwork would be painted on glass approximately six feet wide and three feet high. Larn described his working practice. "The matte studio was long and narrow and consisted of four identical easels permanently fixed to the floor, and the up and down motion of the heavily framed glass paintings was counterbalanced by weights that ran up and down in a boxed-in channel, much like the old sash windows." The glass painting and live action would be combined in an optical printer.

Larn would go on to work on twenty-five feature films including *Dr Zhivago* (1965), *Casino Royale* (1967) and Ray Harryhausen's dinosaurs and cowboys epic *The Valley of Gwangi* (1969).

For a science fiction film, the production is short on model work. One shot that is effective is the Dalek city as seen through the trees of the Skaro forests; not a matte painting but a model of the city. This was placed on set at the furthest end of the stage to create a forced perspective.

ABOVE: The gorge artwork and its subtle addition of lighting helps create the final effect.

BELOW: The Dalek City model as seen in the final film.

MUSIC

Malcolm Lockyer was born in Greenwich, London. He trained initially as an architect but decided to follow his passion for music. His jazz style was at odds with the mysterious and otherworldly Radiophonic Workshop music the BBC had created for the *Doctor Who* series, and which viewers had come to rely on as central to the atmosphere of the show.

The music for the film, then, was another departure from the television series. Subotsky could not agree on the rights for the famous theme, so they went in an entirely different direction. Lockyer had a busy 1965 scoring two other feature films, *Ten Little Indians* and *The Pleasure Girls*. Co-Producer Joe Vegoda had a music publishing company and it would be

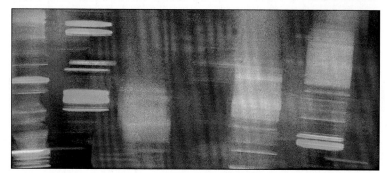

"WHO'S WHO"

Recorded on polydor BM 56021 BY

ROBERTA TOVEY

From the film "DOCTOR WHO AND THE DALEKS"
starring
PETER CUSHING • ROY CASTLE • JENNIE LINDEN • ROBERTA TOVEY
A Regal Films International Release

ultimately his decision to commission Lockyer to write the film's score.

Producer Milton Subotsky had wanted to work the original theme into the film, but money was the stumbling block. "We couldn't get it because they [the BBC] were asking far too much money for it, which was a shame because I didn't like the music for the first film; it was too heavy. I wanted a more action-packed score." The title sequence was a similar story. Subotsky wanted one which was closer to the television version: swirling mists that were originally created by two video cameras outputting visual feedback. Again a price for this was never agreed with the BBC. Instead he shot coloured lights though moving sheets of translucent plastic.

Subotsky had to rush the film through post-production to meet cinema deadlines. Lockyer's music for *Dr. Who* was a 'beat' style of electronic guitar and percussion trendy in the mid-1960s, and instantly dates the film to that period. It does fit with Subotsky's plan to attract a more family-oriented audience.

Two singles were also released based on the score from the film with vocals from young actress Roberta Tovey. Tovey enjoyed the experience, even if it didn't make her a pop star.

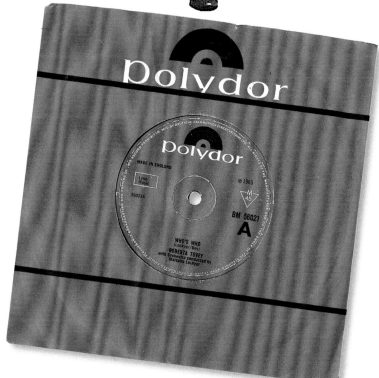

TOP: Commercial for the single release. Photo from Richard Holliss.

ABOVE: The 7" single. Photo from Christopher Hill / The Space Museum.

"Polydor asked me to do a record called *Who's Who?* That was quite fun to do. I went into the studio with the orchestra and cut the record in one take, which was quite frightening at the time. I don't know if it was that much of a success. But it was fun, and sometimes I hear it now and again." Another single was to follow: 'The Eccentric Dr.

Who'/'Daleks and Thals', released in August 1965. This had a busy arrangement of the film's main theme and a B-side with incidental music.

Barry Gray was best known for his work with Gerry Anderson's puppet series. His compositions for *Thunderbirds*, *Captain Scarlet* and *Space: 1999* are amongst the most familiar and beloved television themes of all time. Gray's use of unconventional recording techniques and electronic effects created the science fiction soundscapes that the film needed. He would continue to work with the Daleks, helping on the sequel. Lockyer, however, wasn't asked back; Subotsky was unhappy with the finished score and went in another direction for the second big-screen Dalek adventure.

The first commercial release of the soundtrack would not happen until 2009's double soundtrack set with the Dalek sequel *Invasion Earth* on the Silva Screen Record label. *Doctor Who* television composer and restoration expert Mark Ayres helped unearth the music. Ayres had scoured the vaults of the then Lumière Film Company – later owned by Canal+, and today known as StudioCanal – at Pinewood Studios while making the documentary *Dalekmania*. He uncovered the 35mm magnetic soundtrack elements to the complete score to the first film, and mixed music and sound effects elements for the second film.

POSTERS

Various release posters for the UK and US market were created, and some rare examples from European countries. All heavily feature the Daleks rather than Dr. Who as the stars of the film.

BILL WIGGINS

Bill Wiggins had been creating poster art since the early 1950s. His work for Hammer Films creating posters for *Dracula* (1958), *The Mummy* (1959) and Ray Harryhausen's *The 3 Worlds of Gulliver* (1960) would lead him to work with Amicus Productions and the Dalek films.

Wiggins' colleague Eddie Paul sketched the early design for the poster. Both men worked at Downtown Advertising, where they created campaigns for many films during the 1960s. The finished Dalek poster art measured 18 inches by 24 inches, and was painted on an artboard with gouache, which is more opaque than watercolour paints. They would have had a handful of production stills and sometimes used office colleagues to create a figure's outline, pose or shape.

An original print run of up to 5,000 would have been made. Many would have been pasted onto bus shelters, tube stations and walls, so they were unrecoverable for collectors. A fraction exist today and come with eye-watering prices at auction. Wiggins remained at Downton until his retirement in 1978.

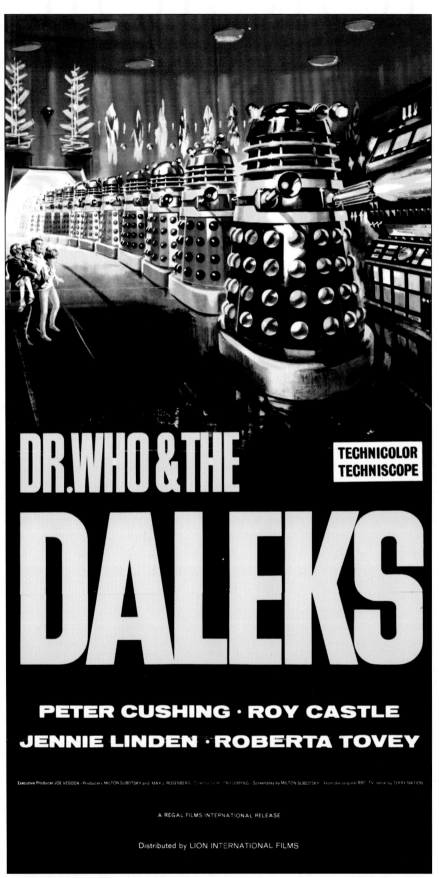

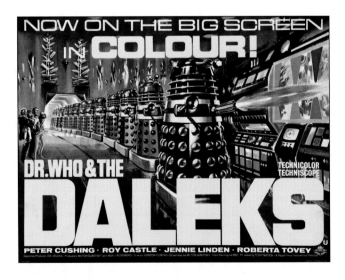

The UK quad poster gives great prominence to the introduction of colour to *Doctor Who & the Daleks*. Dr. Who, Susie, Barbara and Ian are shrunken figures to the far left of the frame. The poster measures 30 in. by 40 in. (76 cm x 102 cm).

The UK one-sheet shows more of the Dalek control room ceiling, previously obscured by the large text font on the quad poster.

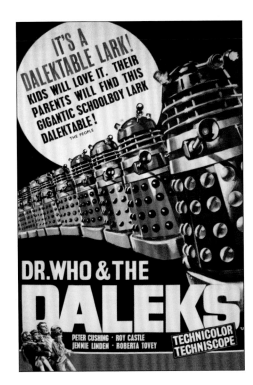

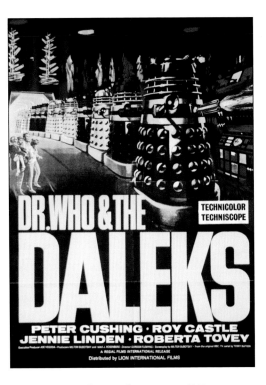

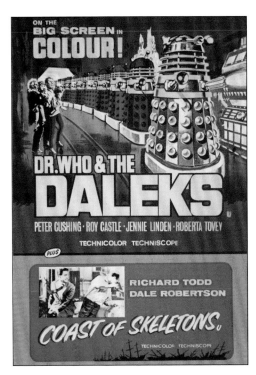

This review poster has one of the few positive film reviews, from the *People* newspaper.

A reissue in 1967: London printers R.J. Wallman created a day-glo yellow, orange and lime green version for cinemas.

This double-bill variant for the UK has different colouring to the main Dalek poster.

This rare Japanese version's title translates as *Doctor Who in the Phantom Dalek's Planet*.

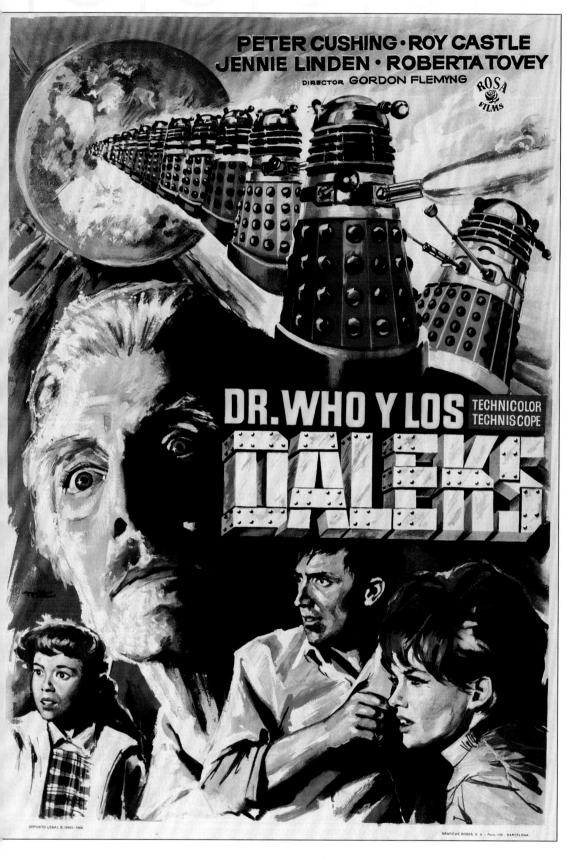

SPAIN

Spanish distributor Rosa Films created all-new artwork placing Dr. Who at the centre of the action. The artist was Macario 'Mac' Gomez, born in 1926. His poster designs included *Ivanhoe* (1952), and *The Ten Commandments* (1956). Contemporary poster artist Tim Doyle told me he is struck by Gomez's art. "This poster has a close up of Cushing's face in the bottom left and Daleks streaming off the Earth in the top. That type of composition is just stunning. It reads like a pulp-novel cover."

AUSTRALIA

This Regal Film Distributors 1966 Australian Daybill poster measures 76 cm by 35 cm. Due to their size, these posters have become rare collector's items; paper shortages after World War II reduced Daybills to these dimensions, and they remained that size until 1980.

US POSTER

This stark blue and black quad poster for the American release uses photomontage and black and white photography to appeal to those more used to threatening science-fiction invasion films, rather than the genteel "Swiss Family Robinson adventure" as described by Milton Subotsky. The US one-sheet has a turquoise hue and retains the same photomontage graphic styling. The artist is unknown.

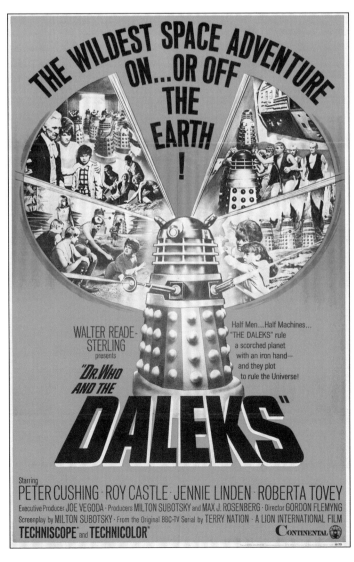

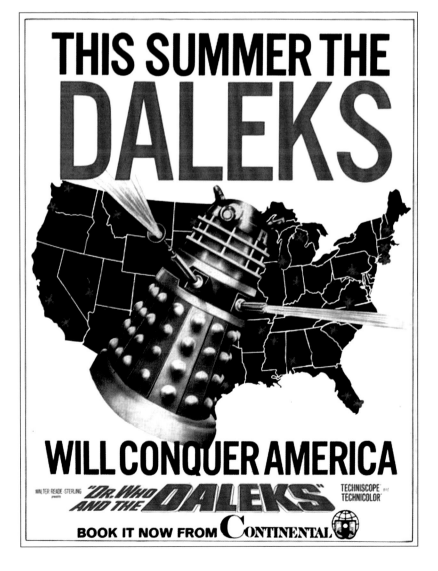

DR. WHO
AND THE
DALEKS

STARRING PETER CUSHING · ROY CASTLE · JENNIE LINDEN · ROBERTA TOVEY

DIRECTED BY GORDON FLEMYNG EXECUTIVE PRODUCER JOE VEGODA PRODUCERS MILTON SUBOTSKY & MAX J. ROSENBERG

DR WHO AND THE DALEKS, Film © 1965 STUDIOCANAL FILMS LTD. All rights reserved

STUDIOCANAL UNDERTHEFLOORBOARDS.COM | DESIGN BY TIM DOYLE MRDOYLE.COM | PRINTING BY NAKATOMIPRINT.COM

TIM DOYLE

When StudioCanal created a new high definition restored version of the film in 2013, Tim Doyle was commissioned to create contemporary sleeve art. Doyle's impressive piece captures the mysterious atmosphere of Dr. Who whilst updating the image for a new market of viewers. Doyle grew up in Dallas, Texas watching the *Doctor Who* television series and Terry Nation's other BBC science-fiction serial, *Blake's 7*.

Doyle told me that he had a free hand in the design. He was told "Doctor Who Peter Cushing movies – GO!" His piece was line art drawn by hand and then scanned and coloured in Photoshop. He watched the films for the first time since he was a child and instantly connected with them again. "I had a profound sense of déjà vu, as I remembered the saturated colours and sets."

Doyle remains a big fan of Bill Wiggins' art. "The originals are quite amazing, honestly. It's hard to think of WHY they would hire me to produce a poster when there's already some brilliant ones! But I'm not going to turn down a chance to work on the Doctor in an official capacity!" He did his research to make sure there was no creative overlap. "It also helps for me as an artist to see how others have 'solved' the design challenge in the past to see if I can build off of that."

TOM CHANTRELL

Chantrell's art was created in 1982 and placed Dr. Who and his fellow travellers at the very centre of the action. This poster resolves the issues of the original poster, where the cast was side-lined in favour of the Daleks. This art was created for the home video release and displays all of Tom Chantrell's brilliance in composition, colour and visualisation. He is best known for his poster for Ray Harryhausen's *One Million Years BC* (1966) and his iconic *Star Wars* (1977) poster, widely believed to be the best, from its original film release.

RELEASE

BELOW: The Daleks hit the Croisette in Cannes.

BELOW RIGHT: A Dalek meets a Beatle.

There was great anticipation amongst the public for the Daleks' big-screen debut. For most producers, making the audience aware of their film's premise is a large part of their advertising costs. With the Daleks, public recognition would not be a problem – but managing the expectations of a Dalek-crazy public would be. Plans were in place to take them on a national tour. The press was the best route to cinemagoers in the 1960s; movie publicity men Harry Pease and Jack Worrow from British Lion Columbia, the film's distributor, headed the project and tried to get as many column inches for the Daleks as possible in the weeks leading up to its release.

On the 8th of April 1965, *Kinematograph Weekly* published details of the PR plan: "After the film has been completed, the set will be re-created in Selfridge's London store for a Dalek Fortnight during which Daleks themselves and all sorts of associated merchandise will be sold. This will coincide with the showing of the film at London's Studio 1 cinema."

The public relations strategy for the film was not just limited to the UK. The Daleks planned to invade Europe too – or the south of France at least. Ten Daleks were taken by truck from Shepperton Studios to the continent, and an eighty-piece brass band saw them on their way with a banner in French reading: "The Daleks Invade Cannes." Once there, they did what anyone would do: toured the various hotels on the Croisette, and even managed to photobomb the Beatle John Lennon who was promoting his new film, *Help!*

The UK press did not embrace the new portrayal of the Doctor or the film's tone, making critical comparisons between film and television series. However, critics did compliment the scope, scale and ambition of the Daleks' first big-screen adventure. *Film Review* said, "most readers will have seen the Daleks on TV, but the limitations of the small screen, with black and white presentations, can give little idea of the impact of the Daleks when seen on a big cinema screen and in breath-taking Technicolor."

There were other positive reviews. "My tip for the latest film craze." – *News of the World*

"Even thrilled someone like me who doesn't give a damn, who's who!" – *Evening Standard*

"The finest creations for children since *Bambi*!" – *Sunday Express*

Films and Filming, in August 1965, was less impressed, dismissing the film as "a patchy piece of Juvenile science fiction." The review heaped praise on the Daleks and the film's design but slammed the cast. "Crude slapstick from Roy Castle and absent-minded bumbling from Peter Cushing." Scorn was also poured on the Thals, "looking and sounding like ballet dancers with their golden hair-dos, heavy eye-shadow and camp speech, [they] must be the wettest tribe on record."

TV21 magazine ran the ultimate Dalek competition with over four hundred and fifty prizes, including three Daleks that had appeared in the film. In addition, there were a series of in-shop promotions for the film, which were standard in the day. For example, the largest retailer on the high street, Woolworths, had window displays for "Dalek Week" with banners in their windows declaring "The Daleks are here and at your local cinema".

The most ambitious and still much-talked-about campaign was at the Lewis department stores, where part of the film's set was recreated along with several Daleks. Roberta Tovey was overwhelmed by the crowd that had gathered. "I remember driving up and seeing hundreds of children queuing. I was surprised. I didn't quite realise so many people were interested in the movies. Apart from being great fans of the TV show, they all wanted to come and see this set that one of the Lewis stores had built for the Daleks. People were queuing for my autograph, and I was getting halfway through it. I couldn't believe people were still coming. I didn't realise there were all these other people out there that wanted to be Susan and wanted to play with the Daleks."

The Lewis department store displays in Birmingham and Manchester were available for three weeks from 27 July 1965. Tovey met fans in the Manchester store on 5 August in Birmingham the next day. A queue greeted her, said to be half mile long. Roberta Tovey's recording debut followed: her single *Who's Who* was released on 13 August through the Polydor record label.

TOP: Dalek shop window banner. Photo from Richard Holliss.

TOP RIGHT & BELOW: Lewis Department Store, Manchester. Photos from Mick Hall

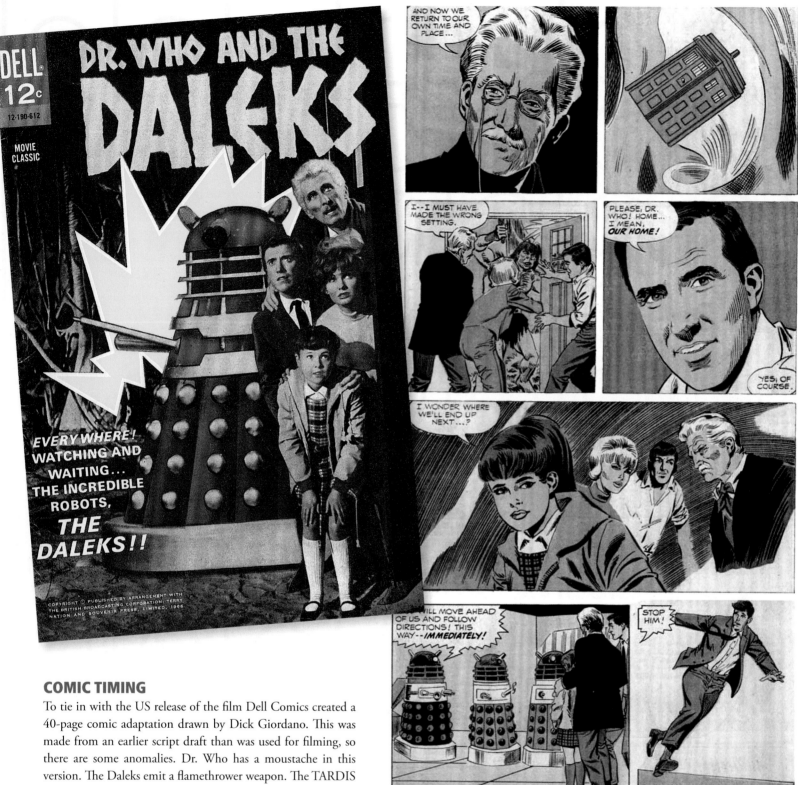

COMIC TIMING

To tie in with the US release of the film Dell Comics created a 40-page comic adaptation drawn by Dick Giordano. This was made from an earlier script draft than was used for filming, so there are some anomalies. Dr. Who has a moustache in this version. The Daleks emit a flamethrower weapon. The TARDIS exterior is coloured green. However the most significant change is the ending, which sees Ian accidentally send the TARDIS off into the past, where they are confronted by a Neanderthal man at the TARDIS doors, and not the Roman army as in the film version. Dell Comics ceased publishing in 1973.

Daily Cinema reported on 30 June 1965 that: "The Daleks have got off to a supercharged start at the box office, giving British Lion Columbia their biggest opening on record." The film opened first at Oxford Street's Studio One cinema, known for its Disney family films. Its eight-week run amassed an impressive £12,000 box office total. It would become one of the top ten box office hits of the year.

DALEKS IN MANHATTAN

The David Tennant serial 'Daleks in Manhattan' in 2007 would officially see the Skaro invaders rolling up and down the streets of New York, but Subotsky got there first, as this rare promotional photo shows: a Dalek on a busy Manhattan street.

The film would receive its British television première on BBC1 on Saturday 1st July 1972 at 7.10pm, with audience viewing figures of 9.9 million making it the most watched *Doctor Who* on television that year.

OPPOSITE: Comic book images from Richard Holliss.

BELOW: Photo from Mick Hall.

DALEKS' INVASION EARTH 2150 A.D. (1966)

DALEKS- INVASION EARTH 2150 A.D.

TECHNICOLOR TECHNISCOPE

THE STORY

Earth is an eerie and sinister place in 2150 A.D. Subjected to a ferocious Dalek invasion, it has been bombarded with meteorites and cosmic rays. Its cities have been smashed. Whole continents wiped out. Human beings turned into living dead men—Robomen—able to act only on radioed instructions from their masters. Other humans have been commandeered to work as slaves in a massive mine in Bedfordshire. Only a small group of resistance fighters holds out in London. . . .

A brilliant scientist, Dr. Who (PETER CUSHING), is transported into the future by a time and space machine. He arrives at the height of the crisis, bringing with him his niece, Louise (JILL CURZON), his grand-daughter Susan (ROBERTA TOVEY), and Tom (BERNARD CRIBBINS), a passing policeman who stumbled into the machine when the controls were already set.

As the party from the Present survey the desolate Future, a Dalek saucer flies in to land in Chelsea. Two resistance fighters, David (RAY BROOKS) and Wyler (ANDREW KEIR), escort the girls to safety in their hide-away. But Dr. Who and Tom are taken as prisoners to the spaceship.

Despite widely broadcast threats of extermination, the morale of the resistance fighters remains high. They gallantly attack the spaceship with hand-made bombs. David helps Dr. Who escape. But Louise—separated from the resistance fighters—is left behind with Tom inside the spaceship. And the Daleks, immune to human bombs, emerge the victors.

Wyler returns to the resistance headquarters to take Susan and their crippled leader, Dortmun (GODFREY QUIGLEY), to greater safety in the suburbs. As they leave they are menacingly surrounded by Daleks. Dortmun hurtles his wheelchair forward and is brutally exterminated. But Susan and Wyler accelerate through in a speeding van.

Forced to run for it when their van is raybombed by the spaceship, Susan and Wyler seek refuge in a cottage, where a family work at clothing the slaves. Desperate for food the family betray them to the Daleks. And the fugitives are taken as prisoners to the Bedfordshire mine.

When the spaceship lands, Louise and Tom escape through a disposal chute. And in the mine they meet Dr. Who and David who have discovered the cause of the invasion. The Daleks' aim is to blast out the planet's metallic core through a fracture in the Earth's crust and pilot it as a spaceship.

But Dr. Who has also discovered the fatal weakness of the metal invaders. Any deviation in the aiming of their bomb would unleash a strong force of magnetic energy and destroy them. . . .

Throwing himself at a master microphone, Dr. Who commands: "Robomen attack Daleks". Under cover of the battle, Tom boards up the main shaft of the mine. And the bomb explodes in the wrong place, at the wrong time.

Sucked into the core of the Earth, the metal invaders are exterminated. And human beings are once again masters of their planet.

THE CAST

Dr. Who	PETER CUSHING	Brockley	PHILIP MADOC
Tom Campbell	BERNARD CRIBBINS	Thompson	EDDIE POWELL
David	RAY BROOKS	Dortmun	GODFREY QUIGLEY
Wyler	ANDREW KEIR	Man on Bicycle	TONY REYNOLDS
Susan	ROBERTA TOVEY	Man with Carrier Bag	BERNARD SPEAR
Louise	JILL CURZON	Young Woman	SHEILA STEAFEL
Wells	ROGER AVON	Old Woman	EILEEN WAY
Conway	KEITH MARSH	Craddock	KENNETH WATSON
Roboman	GEOFFREY CHESHIRE	Robber	JOHN WREFORD
Leader Roboman	STEVE PETERS	Leader Dalek Operator	ROBERT JEWELL

TECHNICAL CREDITS

Length 7,578 feet

Running Time 84 minutes

Reg. No.

Executive Producer	JOE VEGODA
Produced by	MAX J. ROSENBERG and MILTON SUBOTSKY
Directed by	GORDON FLEMYNG
Screenplay by	MILTON SUBOTSKY
	From the B.B.C. Television Serial by TERRY NATION
Additional Dialogue by	DAVID WHITTAKER
Director of Photography	JOHN WILCOX, B.S.C.
Art Director	GEORGE PROVIS
Editor	ANN CHEGWIDDEN
Production Manager	TED WALLIS
Unit Manager	TONY WALLIS
Assistant Director	ANTHONY WAYE
Camera Operator	DAVID HARCOURT
Sound Recordist	BUSTER AMBLER
Continuity	PAMELA DAVIES
Wardrobe Supervisor	JACKIE CUMMINS
Make-up	BUNTY PHILLIPS
Hairdresser	BOBBIE SMITH
Production Secretary	VIVIENNE EDEN
Special Effects	TED SAMUELS
Set Decoration	MAURICE PELLING
Construction Manager	BILL WALDRON
Camera Grip	RAY JONES
Sound Editor	JOHN POYNER
Sound Supervisor	JOHN COX
Music Composed by	BILL McGUFFIE

Colour by TECHNICOLOR Photographed in TECHNISCOPE
AN AARU PRODUCTION
PRODUCED AT SHEPPERTON STUDIOS, ENGLAND

NEW CASTING

The success of *Dr. Who & The Daleks* meant a sequel was inevitable. Subotsky would keep to the same formula and adapt an existing Terry Nation Dalek story from 1964 that had been a success with television viewers. His star Peter Cushing would return in the title role and was ready to be asked. "It was no surprise to me to learn that the first *Doctor Who* film came into the Top 20 box office hits. That's why they made a sequel and spent almost twice as much money on it."

Subotsky would also retain many of the same production personnel, including Director Gordon Flemyng, Cinematographer John Wilcox and Ted Samuels on special effects; but the cast would change. Only Peter Cushing and Roberta Tovey would reprise their roles from the first film. Tovey says talk of a sequel was already in the air during the final days of the first shoot. "Just before we finished shooting the first film, Milton Subotsky asked me would I do another film. He told me Peter Cushing said, "I will do another movie if Roberta will be in it as well." When he told me that, I was thrilled. I was delighted to do another movie."

The storyline of *Invasion Earth* would be much grittier and required new cast members to take on the roles of rebellious humans who refused to be enslaved to the Daleks. Because Jennie Linden was unavailable to return as granddaughter Barbara, a new niece character was created, and this meant no room for Roy Castle as Barbara's love interest.

In an early draft of the script, Barbara was to return. The screenplay opens with Tom Campbell arriving at Dr. Who's house and wanting to make a phone call. The house phone is occupied, and he sees the police call box in the garden and enters. In another mirroring of the first film, the ending of *Invasion Earth* would see Susan letting Tom choose to go forward into the future and then back again into the past. Stock film footage would likely have been employed here, as it was for the first film. A new approach was taken for a more dramatic opening with the jewellery shop robbery sequence.

JILL CURZON AS "LOUISE"

OPPOSITE: Jill Curzon in a publicity shot with a costume designed to catch attention and not entirely accurate to her one in the film.

BELOW: A rare shot of Jill taken in her film costume, flanked by new Daleks created for the sequel. Photo from Mick Hall.

Jill Curzon had worked on series such as *The Champions* (1976) and *The Saint* (1965). She was cast as Dr. Who's niece Louise after meeting with both Subotsky and director Flemyng. "Milton Subotsky was a little bit inspiring. He seemed to like me, but he was very austere, and I didn't know what he thought. I met Gordon Flemyng, who was delightful. I then knew I had the part." Her favourite Dalek co-star was Bernard Cribbins. "He was great fun to work with. I did most of my scenes with him. We had a lot of fun. He's very shy with a good sense of humour." Curzon remembered laughing much of the time working with Cribbins, but there were times when she was anxious too, such as jumping from the Dalek saucer. "One of the most enjoyable scenes was going down the waste chute of the spaceship. We had this vacuum sucking all the sweets from the trays. It was quite frightening. I didn't know how much of the vacuum was going to tear our hair. It wasn't a huge drop, but it was quite hard. You had to make sure you knew how to roll and fall; otherwise, you might break your ankle."

During her time at the studios, she saw other more glamorous shoots, but preferred her Dalek film. "Next door, they were shooting *Casino Royale* (1967) with Ursula Andress, David Niven and hordes of beautiful girls. It was rather fun because I was the only girl going into the *Dr. Who* studio. I felt quite exclusive. Everybody loves the Daleks. At lunchtime, Bernie Cribbins would go off fishing. The rest of us would sit with Ursula Andress and the beautiful girls. We got to know all of them very well indeed. And I think Bernie missed out on a few things there. But he seemed to enjoy fishing better." Cribbins would land a role in *Casino Royale* after shooting wrapped on the Dalek film, playing the role of a British Foreign Office official.

BERNARD CRIBBINS AS "TOM CAMPBELL"

Bernard Cribbins, OBE, has been known to generations of viewers from his film and television roles. His most beloved parts include Albert Perks in *The Railway Children*, the narrator of the BBC children's series *The Wombles* (1973–1975), and a regular guest reader for children's series *Jackanory* from 1966 to 1991. However, Cribbins would be the only actor to play a companion to both big screen and small screen Doctors when he took the role of Wilfred Mott, grandfather to Donna Noble and a temporary companion to the Tenth Doctor played by David Tennant.

I met with Bernard Cribbins at London's Excel Centre in 2013 for the 50th-anniversary celebrations and asked him about his time on the Dalek movie. His introduction to director Gordon Flemyng was during a scene where he thought he was "going to end up on the naughty step", and the director became furious with him. "I had not met the director Gordon Flemyng when I found myself on set doing a scene with the Daleks for the very first time. We were filming a scene on the ramp in the spaceship, and Peter Cushing and I had just been introduced to the Daleks. Bob Jewell was the main Dalek operator, and he is an Australian. When he called out his line, "You will come with us, or you'll be exterminated", he did it in this strong Australian accent. Peter and I couldn't stop laughing. Gordon said, "Come

on guys, pull yourselves together!" but every time the Dalek said the line, we had a fit of giggles. The director swore at me a few times."

Cribbins had worked with Peter Cushing the year before on the remake of *She* (1965) with Ursula Andress and John Richardson. "We had a wonderful time on that. So it was a nice opportunity to work with Peter again, who was great fun." Cribbins was struck by Cushing's take on the Doctor, distinct from the television portrayal. "Peter played him on film as a bubbling old gentleman, and he always looked to me as if he was just finishing a mint, and then he would speak."

Cribbins was offered the leading role of the Doctor himself when the third television Doctor Jon Pertwee was leaving in 1974. "I went along for an interview, and this was when they were looking for someone after Jon Pertwee. I saw producer Barry Letts, and he asked me what I could do. I told him, 'I can ride a horse, I can swim. I was a paratrooper, and I can fight too'. He looked a bit shocked, and he said, 'Oh no, no fighting for the Doctor'. Maybe I lost the job because I said, 'I'm good at fighting', but then, of course, when they cast Tom Baker and you see him on screen, he gives someone a smack and knocks them over. I'd have loved to have been Doctor Who."

RAY BROOKS AS "DAVID"

BELOW: David and Dr. Who inspect the Daleks' plan.

The young rebel role would go to Ray Brooks. He played minor roles in feature films before *Doctor Who* but was best known for his role in British soap opera *Coronation Street* (1964). A long and successful career followed, including Ken Loach's ground-breaking BBC film, *Cathy Come Home* (1966). Much like Bernard Cribbins, Brooks is best remembered for his narration of a children's animated series, the similarly time-travelling *Mr Benn* (1971-1972).

ANDREW KEIR AS "WYLER"

Andrew Keir was seen on screen in big-budget feature films *A Night to Remember* (1958), *Cleopatra* (1963) and Hammer Film's *Dracula: Prince of Darkness* (1966) before his role as Wyler in *Invasion Earth*. He is best remembered for playing Professor Bernard Quatermass in Hammer Films' *Quatermass and the Pit* (1967). He also originated the role of Thomas Cromwell in Robert Bolt's original play of *A Man for All Seasons* (1960).

111 DALEKS' INVASION EARTH 2150 A.D. (1966)
PHILIP MADOC AS "BROCKLEY"

None of the actors who appeared in the two Amicus Dalek films had as many encounters with the Time Lord as Philip Madoc. In *Daleks' Invasion Earth 2150 A.D.*, he plays black-marketeer Brockley, who betrays Dr. Who to the Daleks but is ultimately destroyed for his duplicity – behaviour even the Daleks will not tolerate. He appeared with the Second Doctor Patrick Troughton on television in 'The Krotons' (1968) and again with Troughton in 'The War Games' (1969). His most memorable television *Doctor Who* role is Doctor Solon in the Tom Baker serial 'The Brain of Morbius' (1976).

His final television *Doctor Who* role would be 'The Power of Kroll' (1978).

In a 1990 *Doctor Who Magazine* interview, Madoc recalled his big-screen adventure with Dr. Who. "It was a reasonable part. I mean, it wasn't two lines, and it stood out, in its way. It was clear, you see, that he was a villain. He ended up in a shed being blown up, but that was his fault for not realising that the Daleks don't have a conscience. They're not going to help someone just for [helping them], particularly, and it was enjoyable seeing how the Daleks worked. That in itself was fascinating."

PETER CUSHING

Cushing's performance in the second film may be a reaction to some of the unkind reviews from the first. His eccentricity and comedic performance are muted and he gives a more restrained portrayal than the first film. His screen time is greatly reduced in the sequel too. Both of these factors may, at least in part, be due to him falling ill shortly before principal photography commenced on 31 January 1966.

His fellow cast did not know of Peter Cushing's poor health during the shoot. Roberta Tovey, who played Susie, was unaware even to this day. "People have said this to me before, but at no time did I see anything that would have suggested that. Whether it was because of being the true professional that he was, it never showed when he was on set, and I never knew of him being ill at all."

Subotsky cleared this up when asked many years later. "He became ill and his doctor said he couldn't work, so what we did was to film every single scene that didn't include Peter Cushing. What we did was to pack-strike the set, which means you take it down and put it into storage and put it up again quite quickly. So what we did was to shoot a scene with everyone but Peter, pack that bit away because we needed the studio space, and put it up again when Peter came back. But we only used those parts

of the set we needed to show behind him." Subotsky didn't know what his star's ailment was but did make an insurance claim for £30,000 for the extra days of filming that were required. Cushing himself commented in 1988 on his absence from the shoot. "I was quite ill during much of the shooting and they had to work around me a good deal."

THE SHOOT

RIGHT: The cast carefully navigate a destroyed London.

BELOW: Director Gordon Flemyng blocks out a scene with Cushing and Cribbins.

BELOW RIGHT: Jill Curzon getting advice from director Flemyng on the Dalek saucer set.

Aaru Productions announced the follow up to *Dr. Who & The Daleks* on the 16th of December 1965. It was a return to Shepperton Stage H. As before the film would be shot in the Techniscope 35mm widescreen format in colour. Originally titled simply *The Daleks Invade Earth*, the name of Dr. Who was not part of this or the final title.

It was Joe Vegoda who would ask Milton Subotsky to script and plan the sequel. With a 60% increase in budget to £286,000, more could be achieved visually than in Terry Nation's original six-part 1964 television serial. In 1990 Subotsky admitted to being reticent about making another Dalek film, but he had a favourite of the two. "I think it turned out to be a better picture than the first one. The second film was largely made in the cutting room! It didn't work until we got it there and made it work. But, looking back, I think the second one moved wonderfully."

DIRECTOR'S COMMENTARY

Director Gordon Flemyng knew this was an opportunity to cash in on the first film's success. "People very quickly realised they'd got a money-maker on their hands and the second film was made in a hurry to cash in on it before it stopped." He was positive about the film and was keen to make an impact with the larger budget. "I chose the picture for two good reasons. One – it was offered. Two – I like entertainment pictures. I'm not saying that the message pictures are not good, because they are. The industry is full of very clever people who are doing message pictures and they've every right to do them. By the same token, I've every right to do entertainment pictures. I don't take them any less seriously and I don't think anyone else should."

Inside the confines of the Dalek city the metal monsters could glide gently through each shot. On the war-torn London

streets this would prove a bigger challenge. "We couldn't go very far because we couldn't make the Daleks work. They wouldn't run on anything other than a smooth surface. On the backlot at Shepperton we could put down camera tracking for them to run on and prepare the set accordingly. In the film, if you see a Dalek moving through rubble, the rubble is either in the foreground or the background. Hopefully the audience doesn't realise this and the trick works."

ABOVE: The full main cast reunite for a rare exterior shoot, on the backlot of Shepperton Studios.

SEQUEL DALEKS

The Daleks' colour changes here bring them more in line with their television cousins, with large black bases and a blue and silver colour scheme with aluminium neck slats. In addition, there was a colour livery amongst the commander-level Daleks in gold, black and red.

ART DIRECTOR

A new art director would take over from Bill Constable. George Provis created a bleaker and more lived-in environment. The interior of the Dalek command spaceship saucer lacked the multi-coloured artistry of Constable's plastic-sculpted Dalek City. The more sombre and austere tone of the film is reflected in the production design. With larger sets to dress and less time to create bespoke designs, Provis relied heavily on hired prop pieces from a prop house, including The Trading Post, already a standard port of call for the *Doctor Who* television series design teams.

Thirty major sets were created by George Provis and his art department team for the film. Provis had worked in science fiction before on the Granada Television special *Seven Steps to the Moon*, which depicted space travel and the future in a realistic style. Provis told *Daily Cinema Magazine* in 1966 that the second Dalek film would allow for "an unencumbered imaginative approach."

ABOVE: A larger budget allowed for a more elaborate home for the Daleks.

NEW TARDIS

As a response to some critics of Bill Constable's unconventional design flourishes for the first film's TARDIS, Provis would create a tidier, practical design for his interior, more in keeping with the television series. As a result, much of what appears here looks like hired props that have been dressed into the space by set decorator Maurice Pelling. Dr. Who's monitor, where he views the aftermath of the jewellery heist, is the closest this new design comes to its small-screen cousin.

TOP RIGHT: TARDIS photo from Mick Hall.

BELOW: A new TARDIS set and an unexpected visitation.

DALEK SAUCER EXTERIOR

In place of the Skaro forest and Dalek city would be an impressive 120-foot Dalek saucer that has landed in the centre of London. The set comprised a section of the saucer and the surrounding desolate, ravaged buildings. This entire construction was housed inside Stage H, where again lighting controls meant continuity of shooting, more so than on an exterior set or the studio backlot. A portion of the underside of the Dalek saucer was built, and in this rare photography you can see where the top of the sound stage starts and the saucer finishes. It would be enhanced in size and grandeur by an impressive Gerald Larn matte painting. The ramp of the saucer would prove difficult for the Dalek operators. Many reported leg lacerations from the more athletic moves required, well beyond those required in the tight confines of a small television studio set.

DALEK SAUCER INTERIOR

Stage H would be the setting for all of the Dalek ship interior shots, including the multi-level area above the mine shaft for the film's climactic confrontation. It was a strongly-constructed set that would take Daleks on a perilously narrow route around the command area and the open mineshaft; this at least had a barrier. Due to the Dalek operators' limited view from inside their machines, this design would undoubtedly need a safety bar today to prevent accidents. At the top of the set, on a pulley system, sits a giant red bomb. This whole design would have been the perfect design for a Dalek playset for children.

There is some hand-held cinematography here, which helps add to the drama. This was likely done for a more practical reason, as the large dolly used for the heavy Mitchell BNC camera could not be manoeuvred through the narrow passages of the set. Inside its blimp housing, the camera would weigh approximately five hundred pounds.

CENTRE: The top of the set is visible in this shot of the Roboman conversion unit.

ABOVE: Bernard Cribbins, 1st AD Anthony Waye and Gordon Flemyng discuss a shot on the Dalek Saucer set.

DESTROYING LONDON

The central set would be built inside, depicting the bombed-out London streets. A painted cyclorama would create the illusion of the outside world and reach high up into the lighting grid of the sound stage, as you will see in these never-before-published images. Dotted around the set are pristine posters advertising Sugar Puffs cereal from the Quaker Oats Company. This product placement was part of a sponsorship deal to help boost the budget of the film. The breakfast cereal would become an integral part of the marketing campaign for the film's release.

OPPOSITE TOP: The impressive London City interior set. Photo from Colin Young. Colourisation by Clayton Hickman.

DALEK COUNTDOWN

The Rels clock, which counted down the minutes to total destruction of the earth's core, would not be out of place in a Sean Connery James Bond film from the era. It is a hired prop from The Trading Post and used in various film and TV projects, including two future *Doctor Who* stories, 'The War Games' (1966) and 'The Underwater Menace' (1967). In 2021 The Prop Store auctioned this Dalek countdown-to-destruction clock, which measures 46 centimetres by 46 centimetres by 15 centimetres. Thanks to Prop Store for sharing previously unpublished images for this book.

OPPOSITE: Rare image from the shoot, with a cameraman clearly visible in shot on the right. Photo from Mick Hall.

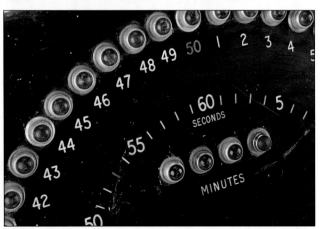

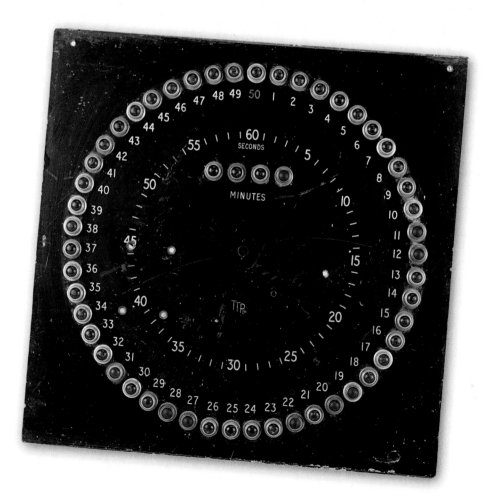

LOCATIONS

OPPOSITE: Dr. Who and David escape the Daleks down a manhole.

BELOW: The Daleks take over the backlot street set at Shepperton Studios.

BELOW RIGHT: A dummy stand-in for actor Godfrey Quigley, who played Dortmun, confronts the Daleks for the final time.

LONDON STREETS

The studio-bound shoot of the first film was a result of the tight budget and fast shooting required. Locations are always more challenging to manage, and shooting takes longer. Whilst it appears that this film was shot around London and in the countryside, it wasn't. Most studios have a standing set of a street: all of the major Hollywood studios would have various streets on their backlots for different periods and multiple television and film productions. The existing street set is first seen at Shepperton during the daring jewel heist in the pre-title sequence with Bernard Cribbins. The first explicit daylight scene is when Susan and Wyler escape in a small van,

passing Daleks as they run from the city. By then, it is one hundred and eighty-four years later, and the city is looking the worse for wear. This standing street set had been redressed to make it more anonymous than its previous 'performances' as a contemporary New York street in the Warren Beatty romantic comedy *Promise Her Anything* (1965) and the 18th Century backdrop for *The Amorous Adventures of Moll Flanders* (1965). Art Director George Provis chooses to dress down the streets and create a drab post-war look that 1960s audiences would have been familiar with from the bombed-out London of the Blitz.

LONDON SEWERS

LONDON SEWERS

The workshops of Shepperton Studios were also dressed with existing interior street set pieces for Dr. Who's night-time escape from the Daleks with David into the sewers.

TUBE STATION

Provis does embellish the future London street by creating a new tube train entrance for Embankment Station. This would prove to be prescient. When the station was opened in 1870, the station was called Charing Cross. In 1974 the station was renamed Charing Cross Embankment. It would not be until 1976 that it became known simply as Embankment.

REAL LOCATIONS

There were a handful of actual locations outside of the Shepperton Studios estate of buildings and lane-ways that were used in the final film. Just outside of the studios was Newfield Bendy Toys Factory. This provided the backdrop to Dr. Who and Tom's first investigation of the destroyed London location. It would lead to the dramatic stunt of Tom nearly falling to his death when he walks through a door that has a fifty-foot drop on the other side. This stunt was completed back on Stage H at Shepperton.

ABOVE: A dangerous stunt that would not be allowed today.

DALEK MINE

The entrance to the mine was also within the confines of the Shepperton Studios backlot. Part of the landscape had a depression that was modified to look like the entrance to the mine. Next to the cabin where the traitorous Brockley comes to an explosive end, two replica aircraft engines from a Vickers Vimy are dressed into the setting. These had been created by Dalek craftsmen Shawcraft Models on a replica of the plane, most likely for a previous film production.

BELOW: Earthlings who are not converted to Robomen are enslaved at the Daleks' mining complex in Bedfordshire.

THE THAMES

The most iconic shot from the film, in which Dr. Who is faced with his mortal enemy once again, was shot by the Thames. This rare photo shows a platform constructed for actors Peter Cushing and Bernard Cribbins to stand safely on. On the bottom right, a technician guides a cable that is pulling the Dalek from the water. This was filmed in Battersea, whilst the original television serial had the Dalek emerge close to Hammersmith Bridge, seven miles away.

Gordon Flemyng described the scene: 'We laid tracks down into the water when the tide was out and positioned a weighted Dalek on them, attached to a line. We then waited for the tide to come in and pulled the Dalek out of the water using the line." The riverbank was also used as the basis for the matte painting by Gerald Larn showing the devastated London cityscape.

BELOW: The only real location shoot for the cast in the film. Colourisation by Clayton Hickman.

CUTTING ROOM DALEKS

Subotsky has always claimed that this film was made in the cutting room. In an exclusive interview with Richard Holliss for *Doctor Who Monthly*, he explained. "We were dubbing the picture, even though they hadn't finished cutting the ending. As it was, it made no sense. There was one chunk of story followed by another when really the scenes should have been intercut to build tension. Ann Chegwidden was the editor on the movie, I simply went through the footage and said to Ann 'look don't argue, just splice as I hand you the pieces and we'll see how it turns out' because there was no time to discuss it. We just locked up the last reel and then dubbed. The ending of *Daleks' Invasion Earth* was made in the cutting room!"

STUNTS

The first film had few stunts. The film's explosive finale was the most dangerous scene, as Dalek operator on the first film Bryan Hands explained to me. "Roy Castle shouts at the Daleks, and they swing around firing at their control panel, and it explodes with all these pyrotechnics. They used a body double for Roy Castle. But they said to us Daleks. 'Oh, you'll be alright there'. So we just sat there with all these explosions going off all around us. I think health and safety was not a prime consideration. It was quite exciting."

No one was hurt on the first film, but several were on the sequel, including a fall resulting in a severe accident for one of the film industry's leading stuntmen. Eddie Powell had been a stand-in and stunt double for Christopher Lee as Dracula, and played the lead creature in some key scenes in Ridley Scott's *Alien* (1979). In *The Omen* (1976) he was attacked by Rottweilers, and in *Jason and the Argonauts* (1963) he took a tumble from the Argo as the ship is turned over in the sea by the giant Talos. He has fallen from great heights and been set on fire. However, it would be a routine stunt in the film that would nearly cost him his life.

The scene involved a daring escape from the Daleks at the foot of the Saucer's ramp. On *Invasion Earth* Powell was the Stunt Co-ordinator responsible for sixteen stunt performers. "I run over the rubble up the side of the building, and I have to run along the joist, and one of the joists has been rigged so that on a special effects guys tripping it, it collapses, and I sort of go into a fall. The trouble was that he's supposed to trip it as I'm putting my foot on it too, so I can position myself for the fall to roll and land on my back. What happened was he tripped it too soon. I went through the air with one foot down and landed on my foot on the awning first, which twisted my ankle and busted something there."

A shot of Powell's character dead was needed, but the pain was severe, and he was unable to lie still. Powell had broken his ankle and was rushed to the hospital. He was back on set the same afternoon with crutches and his foot in plaster. They needed to get a shot of him on the ground being exterminated by the Daleks, and in this still image from the archives, you can see Powell's plastered foot hidden under his other leg.

The most breath-taking stunt was not performed by Powell but by a fellow stuntman, Jackie Cooper, who doubled for Bernard Cribbins as his character opened the door to a fifty-foot fall. "All he had was a very tight strap around his wrist. Nowadays, you would have a full body harness on underneath, which goes up through the arm wire coming down through and is as safe as houses. But he felt quite confident to go for that wrist strap."

Powell would later appear on screen as a stuntman in the Fourth Doctor's adventure, 'The Deadly Assassin', in 1976.

ABOVE RIGHT: Powell's cast is just visible under his left leg.

ROBO STUNTS

Powell's brother helped to try and bring an end to the Dalek's plan to take over the Earth by lending a hand in a final scene on the Dalek Saucer by the mine. "My brother, Joe, was an ex-SAS Commando. He had to fight one of the Daleks and ends up with a Dalek throwing him over into this deep bomb hole where they're going to blast something way down in the depths of the Earth. If you watch the film closely, you will see that as he goes over, he takes one of the claws of the Dalek and then the very next scene, magically, the Dalek has got it back again. Must be something to do with regeneration there somewhere." This rare unit still captures the moment when the claw falls with Joe Powell.

ABOVE & BELOW:
Falling backwards is considered one of the most dangerous stunts.

STUNT GIRL

Amazingly, a dangerous stunt involved a vital member of the cast and the youngest person on the shoot, Roberta Tovey. "I remember we had to do a scene in the van driving along escaping from the Daleks. They had a double for Andrew Keir, who was driving. Eddie Powell did that. But they couldn't have the double for me. I had to sit in the van the whole time. We were trundling along about ninety miles an hour. I used to think that I was going to get thrown out at the side as I didn't even have a seat belt."

Eddie Powell admits to the drive being a challenge. "There's a piece of muddy road I had to go along with, but I knew I had to hit speed to make it look anything at all. So I had the feeling I was going to be sliding all over the place, which it did. But I managed to control it." Actor Andrew Keir who played Wyler damaged his wrist in the scene where he pushes a hole in the windscreen during the escape.

After surviving the drive, Tovey had another brush with danger. "We had to do the shot where the van gets attacked by the flying saucer. We had one take to do that. We drove into the scene with the van all wired up with explosives and had to jump out and run. They ignited the detonators and blew the van up. We did all that for real."

MODEL EFFECTS

OPPOSITE: The Dalek saucer ready for filming with nylon wires clearly visible.

BELOW: Through careful lighting the wires were not visible in most of the final filmed sequences.

With the increase in the budget, there was the chance for more ambitious special visual effects photography.

DALEK SAUCER

Ted Samuels designed, built and shot the model Dalek Saucer in flight. Samuels was head of the Shepperton Studios Special Effects Department, where he designed and oversaw the construction of the four-foot-wide model. It was flown simply on wires. The lighting is crucial to hide the wires and give the illusion of flight. It was relatively lightweight despite having a battery-powered motor to revolve the centre and light the many porthole windows.

Lighting continuity and visual scale are the two significant challenges facing the model photography unit. Creating a large Dalek saucer and shooting in daylight helped with both.

However, the model would get blown around from the end of the polearm boom it was attached to in the wintry Shepperton skies of February 1966. In the brief scene where the saucer flies low to shoot at Wyler and Susan's van, the model was composited with the live-action in an optical printer.

Samuels directed the dramatic demise and destruction of the Dalek saucer. According to writer Richard Holliss, Samuels spent five hours wiring up the explosives and covered the action with four cameras filming simultaneously. He also exploded the small laboratory model perched on the hill above the mine. Over the years Holliss has become fascinated with this singular piece of Dalek technology. He let me in on Ted Samuels' filming secrets for the final shot of the saucer. "Samuels' team built a breakaway model of the saucer that was filled with pyrotechnics and substituted it in the penultimate frame so that the actual model wasn't damaged. The saucer turned up in *The Body Stealers* (1969) before being sold off in a Shepperton Studios prop auction in the early 1970s. I saw a clip on TV at the time and immediately recognized the Dalek spaceship sitting on a table among dozens of other props. As I recall, it had a price tag attached to one of the back fins, but I have no idea what the reserve was."

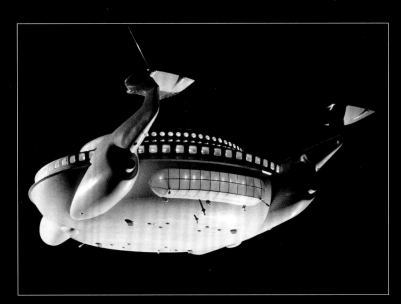

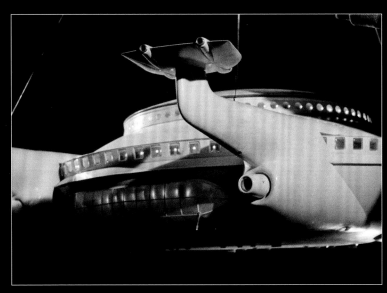

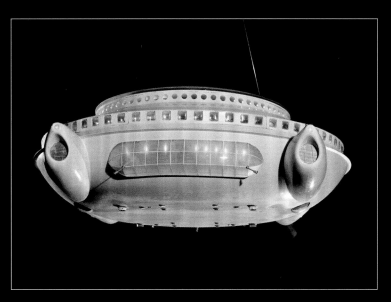

DR. WHO & THE DALEKS : THE OFFICIAL STORY OF THE FILMS

DALEK DESTRUCTION

Samuels also created the many shots of Dalek deaths that happen in quick succession during the film's explosive finale as the Earth's magnetic pull drags the Daleks to their end. In this video age, we can watch the film a frame at a time to see that Samuels has used some toy Daleks intercut with the full-sized ones from the main shoot. For the crumpling Dalek effect, a rubber mould was made, inflated and painted. It was then detonated from behind with a small explosive to give the shrivelling effect.

Director Gordon Flemyng knew that the special effects team had a tough assignment for the sequel. "I remember that those scenes were complex and difficult because we had limited facilities. We couldn't keep reshooting until we were totally happy. There were a number of model shots which we could afford to do a couple of times but after that we had to fake it. Although the film had a relatively bigger budget than the first, it was mostly eaten up by the sheer number of effects and the location work."

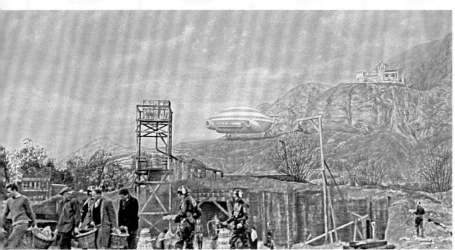

MATTE PAINTINGS

Gerald Larn would return and create five matte paintings. Visual effects historian Domingo Lizcano has shared his interview with Larn discussing the challenges of the main Dalek saucer matte painting. "What I am sure of is that I had to visualize and paint the crashed flying saucer matte very early in the production of the film. At that point, the flying saucer model (later to be filmed on our effects stage) had not yet been made. So the only saucer reference I had to work from was a selection of scale drawings being prepared for the construction of the model. I can remember it being a tricky operation trying to design the craft from those drawings and at the same time ensure the saucer sat convincingly on the circular underbelly built on the set. It ended up being a series of compromises with which I was never entirely satisfied."

When the matte painting was introduced in the film, the problem of combining live-action with a painting was often solved by having the painting on set or on location and shooting directly through it as the actors are placed into the scene in the distance. Unfortunately, the results were sometimes unusable. To control both environments, Larn would use an optical printer. The optical printer is a large mechanical device that takes two pieces of exposed film and allows them to be projected separately onto an unexposed third strip of film by pointing directly at a film camera. The advantage of placing two images together is that it helps create the illusion of size and scale when

a model or painting is placed with actors filmed on location or on set. However, each time an image is passed through this process, there is a loss of quality, as the film degrades a generation each time, so it needs to be used with care. This image of the Westheimer Company optical printer used on the original Star Trek television series, courtesy of Visual Effects Director Mark Wolf, is a good example of the machine that would have been available to Larn at the time of shooting.

Larn's work on the film would also include painting the Dalek saucer at the mine and in other more discreet areas. "There was quite a lot of matte work involved in the other shots, adding and topping up ruined buildings."

Neither Gerald Larn nor Ted Samuels was credited for their work on the Dalek films.

ABOVE: Brightly-lit daytime shots are a bigger challenge for visual effects than the darkness of space and star fields.

BELOW: The complex lacing of an optical printer leaves little room for error.

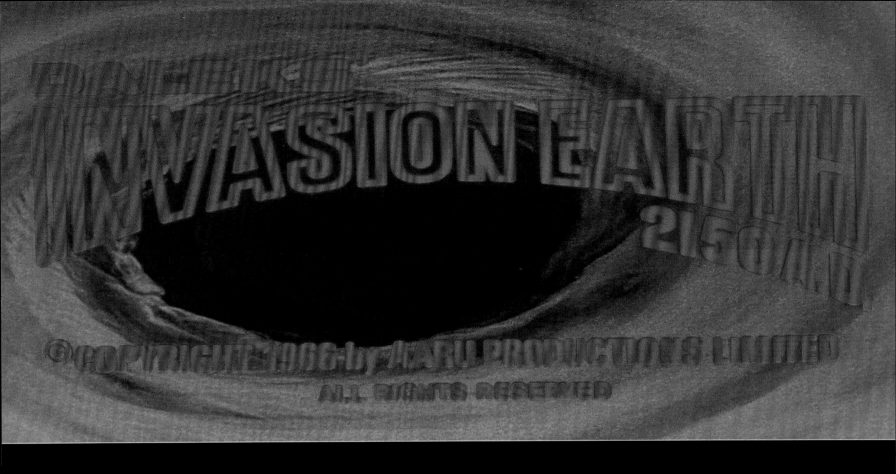

TITLE SEQUENCE

One of the last visual effects to be completed for the film was its opening title sequence. This looks suspiciously closer to the television series. Milton Subotsky was asked about this swirling tunnel effect. "That was very simple and done in the effects studio. It was nothing more than a series of paints and oils going down a drain. A simple and cheap effect. Is that what you wanted? No! I would have liked the BBC titles!"

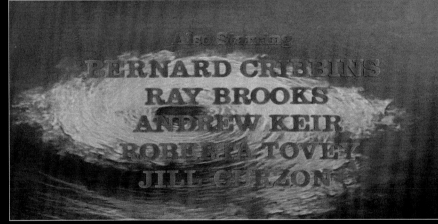

MUSIC

Milton Subotsky was keen to change direction with the music for the sequel. Gone were the lyrical tones of the family-friendly Malcolm Lockyer score, and in came a faster-paced, brassy-sounding, jazz-infused score from Bill McGuffie. John Barry had scored four James Bond films by 1966, and his music influenced some of McGuffie's action set pieces. In addition, Barry Gray returned from the first film to add his usual mix of electronic sound effects to the music.

McGuffie was an accomplished pianist, which was all the more miraculous given that he had lost the third finger on his right hand in an accident when he was eight years old, trapping it in the doors of a telephone kiosk. The film opens with classical music, Bach's 'Toccata and Fugue in D minor'. This has been a popular piece used in many post-war science fiction films, from *20,000 Leagues Under the Sea* (1954) to *Rollerball* (1975).

McGuffie created a variation on this Bach work and released it in February 1967, calling it *Fugue for Thought*. This, along with the surviving music elements, was released in 2009 by Silva Screen Records on CD and Vinyl. This would be the very first release of the scores.

As with the first film, the score for *Invasion Earth* was lovingly restored by Mark Ayres. However, the entire score was not found in StudioCanal's Pinewood film archive. Only the M&E track (Music and Effects) produced for foreign-language dubbing of the film was uncovered. The full isolated music score track has yet to be found.

Mark Ayres brought his expertise to bear to create the best sounding version of both films for their première music release. "The tapes were not in the best condition, with prominent noise, distortion, dropouts and variations in levels, but I felt that, with a bit of TLC and a lot of digital tweaking, an album would be possible."

On Record Store Day on April 16th 2011, Silva Screen released a limited edition 7-inch vinyl with a selection of tracks and dialogue from both films for a limited five hundred copy pressing. McGuffie would score several feature films, including the British horror film *Corruption* (1968), starring Peter Cushing in the role of a doctor again, albeit this time a crazed plastic surgeon with a lethal surgical laser.

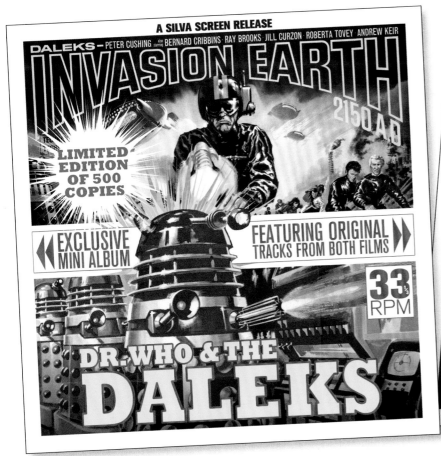

POSTERS

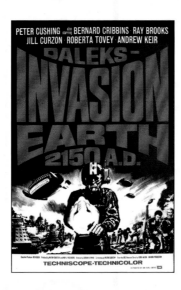

BILL WIGGINS

The sequel's poster artwork would see the return of Bill Wiggins. His art became the basis for many of the variants that followed in 1966 and for the film's reissues. Wiggins minimizes both the Daleks and Dr. Who to place the Roboman at the centre of the image.

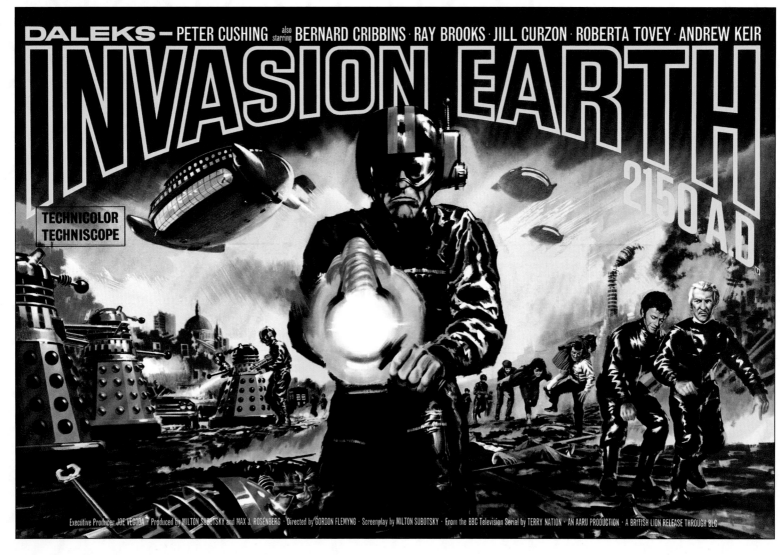

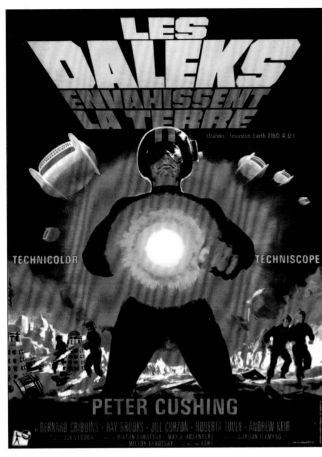

MICHEL LANDI

The French poster artist Michel Landi takes a similar approach with his design here.

CHRIS ACHILLÉOS

Chris Achilléos' iconic artworks for the *Doctor Who* Target Books novelisations have become fan favourites over the years. For his cover of the television adaptation, he chose the design of the film Dalek saucer as the looming presence over the London landscape. This cover was first seen on 24 March 1977. The image remains the copyright of the late Chris Achilléos and is reproduced here with his kind permission. He explained to me in a new interview about the change of style. "I did it because I could not find any photography from the BBC for the flying saucer, and I was working to a tight deadline. I saw the film Dalek saucer in a magazine and used that instead. The publisher has never noticed; the author never said anything. And the book sold a million." A book of his collected art is now available from Candy Jar Books: *Kklak! The Doctor Who Art of Chris Achilléos*.

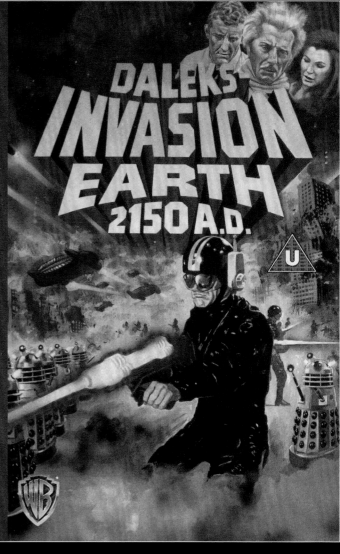

Dr. Who is transported by the TARDIS to a desolated future Earth under cosmic attack by the vengeful Daleks. Whole continents have been wiped out and humans turned into Robomen — living dead slaves!
The evil Daleks plan to blast out the Earth's core with an atomic bomb and pilot the conquered planet as a giant spaceship. Only the underground resistance movement stands in the way of total Dalek control and extermination...

Daleks —
Invasion Earth 2150 A.D.
Starring PETER CUSHING
Also Starring BERNARD CRIBBINS, RAY BROOKS, JILL CURZON, ROBERTA TOVEY, ANDREW KEIR
Screenplay by MILTON SUBOTSKY From the BBC TV serial by TERRY NATION
Produced by MILTON SUBOTSKY and MAX J. ROSENBERG Directed by GORDON FLEMYNG

WARNER HOME VIDEO

Running Time: 81 mins COLOUR PAL/ENGLISH LANGUAGE

Programme content © Aaru Productions Limited 1966. All Rights Reserved.

DALEKS INVASION EARTH 2150 A.D.

U

VHS PAL

PES 38025

TOM CHANTRELL

Chantrell's second home-video commissioned piece from 1982 puts the Roboman at the centre of the composition. As in Chantrell's *Dr. Who & The Daleks* piece, using wrap-around text for the film's title, Chantrell again makes excellent use of the title text block. Traditionally this would be left blank for a typography layout designer, but Chantrell makes it part of the drama as it breaks through the fiery skyline. The film's cast also gets more prominence than in Bill Wiggins' original cinema release artwork.

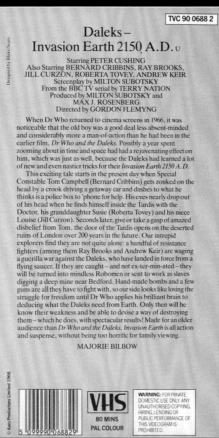

TVC 90 0688 2

Designed by Blake Sears

Daleks —
Invasion Earth 2150 A.D. U
Starring PETER CUSHING
Also Starring BERNARD CRIBBINS, RAY BROOKS,
JILL CURZON, ROBERTA TOVEY, ANDREW KEIR
Screenplay by MILTON SUBOTSKY
From the BBC TV serial by TERRY NATION
Produced by MILTON SUBOTSKY and
MAX J. ROSENBERG
Directed by GORDON FLEMYNG

When Dr Who returned to cinema screens in 1966, it was noticeable that the old boy was a good deal less absent-minded and considerably more a man-of-action than he had been in the earlier film, *Dr Who and the Daleks*. Possibly a year spent zooming about in time and space had had a rejuvenating effect on him, which was just as well, because the Daleks had learned a lot of new and even nastier tricks for their *Invasion Earth 2150 A.D.*

This exciting tale starts in the present day when Special Constable Tom Campbell (Bernard Cribbins) gets zonked on the head by a crook driving a getaway car and dashes to what he thinks is a police box to 'phone for help. His eyes nearly drop out of his head when he finds himself inside the Tardis with the Doctor, his granddaughter Susie (Roberta Tovey) and his niece Louise (Jill Curzon). Seconds later, give or take a gasp of amazed disbelief from Tom, the door of the Tardis opens on the deserted ruins of London over 200 years in the future. Our intrepid explorers find they are not quite alone: a handful of resistance fighters (among them Ray Brooks and Andrew Keir) are waging a guerilla war against the Daleks, who have landed in force from a flying saucer. If they are caught – and not ex-ter-min-ated – they will be turned into mindless Robomen or sent to work as slaves digging a deep mine near Bedford. Hand-made bombs and a few guns are all they have to fight with, so our side looks like losing the struggle for freedom until Dr Who applies his brilliant brain to deducing what the Daleks need from Earth. Only then will he know their weakness and be able to devise a way of destroying them – which he does, with spectacular results! Made for an older audience than *Dr Who and the Daleks*, *Invasion Earth* is all action and suspense, without being too horrific for family viewing.

MAJORIE BILBOW

THORN EMI VIDEO   THORN EMI VIDEO

STARRING PETER CUSHING

DALEKS INVASION EARTH 2150 A.D.

TVC 90 0688 2

ITALIAN POSTER

The artist here is legendary poster designer Renato Casaro. His other fantasy and science fiction art work would include *Flash Gordon* (1980), *Conan the Barbarian* (1982) and *Dune* (1984).

SYRIAN POSTER

A rare variation on the Wiggins design appeared in Syria in the early 1970s. This poster was found in Damascus. This may be a partial image as both the Daleks and date 2015 AD are missing here; however, the layout matches other Syrian and Egyptian portrait cinema posters from the time. [photo credit: Colin Young]

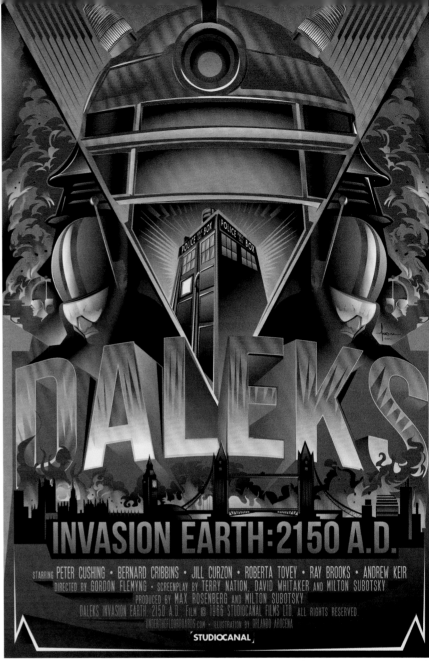

ORLANDO AROCENA

New artwork on the 2015 limited edition Steelbook Blu-Ray release was from renowned vector graphics illustrator Orlando Arocena. He shared his main image here, with the Daleks centre stage, and showed me his unused art for a Roboman cover. I spoke with Orlando Arocena about the films and his inspiration for these two stunning pieces of art. "When you have a particular property that's very well known, the studio sometimes wants to create something that helps refresh the image but is safe. It is more freeing when my interpretation comes through without sacrificing the core personality of the film."

Arocena took a fresh approach but was a fan of British science fiction television and films. "I do enormous research, and I looked back to be inspired by Bill Wiggins' art. I like to look back at British television and movies from that genre and timeframe. I remember seeing *Space 1999* promotional posters in the subway in New York. A lot of that British sci-fi had a substantial influence on the direction I was going on for this new Dalek piece. I tried to make sure that I didn't fall into adopting too much of that visual equity or style and that I was able to translate it into my design aesthetic."

Arocena's advanced graphic design technique is more in line with the future promised by the Dalek films. "Sometimes, I'll do a very quick doodle. On this project, I jumped into vector graphics. I try to do it digitally and allow the spontaneity to be part of the energy that goes into the piece."

After collecting visual reference materials, Arocena needed to bring his originality to the art whilst respecting what has gone before. "Certain titles are so pop-culture ingrained and have been done by so many artists that you've got to find a unique way to bring that passion back to that particular property. So I'll just jump right in and start doing what I call vector freestyle, meaning that there's no net, and you're just having to formulate something out of nothing. But I still keep a cognizance, a sense of what it is that you want to try to hit."

The solitary Roboman image struck a creative chord with Arocena "I liked the design essence of the Robomen, their helmets and their leather-clad, stoic, angry faces. I also wanted to pay tribute to them with the poster. I'm delighted with it because it was one of my first actual commissions."

ABOVE LEFT: Arocena's unused Roboman artwork.

ABOVE RIGHT: Arocena's Dalek poster has a 1960s styling.

RELEASE

When this sequel went before the censors, the stronger violence and more adult themes were noted, but the film would still go on to receive the "U" rating needed for as many people as possible to see it in cinemas:

The British Board of Film Censors gave their verdict: "Violence: There is a chaotic fight scene involving many characters all fighting at the same time in which it is implied that a man is stabbed in the stomach with a knife. A knife is then thrown at a man who is high up on another level, and the man can be seen falling with the knife in his stomach. The actual knife impact is not shown. We also see men being killed by the jets of steam from the Daleks, but they die with no injury detail. There are a few truncheon blows but these are all brief and not clearly visible."

The filmmakers were keen to attract an older audience, too, and part of the marketing played to this. Jill Curzon recalls her Dalek photo shoot: "I did a lot of bikini shots and glamour poses and things for various magazines and newspapers."

As before, the Daleks themselves were the centrepiece of the marketing. The Quaker Oats Company partly sponsored the film for their

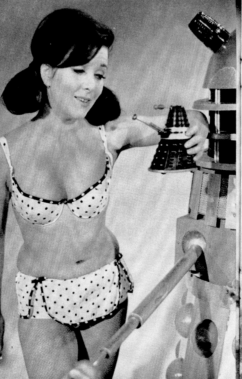

The Day She Fell For A Dalek

It was in London in 1941, when the city was going up in large lumps of stone and little bits of brick, that JILL CURZON was born. She remembers the day she was born, not because of the bombs but because they had dried egg omelette for breakfast in the maternity ward.

Jill went off dried egg from then on, but she grew up into quite a dish all the same and decided she wanted to be an actress.

She went into films and subsequently her agent said, "They want you to look histrionic and sexy in a film about the Daleks." And Jill, who was always too busy to watch the telly on a Saturday afternoon and didn't know what a Dalek looked like, said "Oh, do you mean a community of Greek fishermen? How fabulous?"

She found out later that the Daleks were just a lot of mechanical monsters, but absolutely cute for all that, and you can see here just how they bowled her over. The day she walked onto the set she said, "I'll have that one, he's a darling."

27

Sugar Puffs cereal. As part of the deal, three original film prop Daleks were given away via a competition on cereal packets. It is believed that up to 3.5 million promotional packs of cereal had gone out to shops by the beginning of August 1967.

The competition would run for six months, allowing for plenty of time to become a regular Sugar Puffs consumer. There were 500 runners-up prizes of Louis Marx toy Daleks. To win the competition, entrants would need to put a list of the skills required to fight the Daleks in the correct order along with a final question in your own words. "I think Sugar Puffs would help me fight the Daleks because…" There was no limit to the number of times you could enter, so long as each application was accompanied by two "guarantee panels" from the side of the competition packs of cereal. According to Frank Ratcliffe in *Kinematograph* in July 1965, the campaign was costing £50,000.

ABC Magazine revealed the winner, ten-year-old John Streeter, "who was presented with his formidable prize at ABC's Astoria Cinema, Brighton. But as John lived 25 miles away, the journey was accomplished by van." Full-size Daleks from the film went on another tour of the country to aid the PR effort. Afterwards, some were returned to Shepperton where the child cast of the new music *Oliver!* (1968) were photographed

ABOVE & BELOW:
Sugar Puffs advertising was impervious to the Dalek attack.

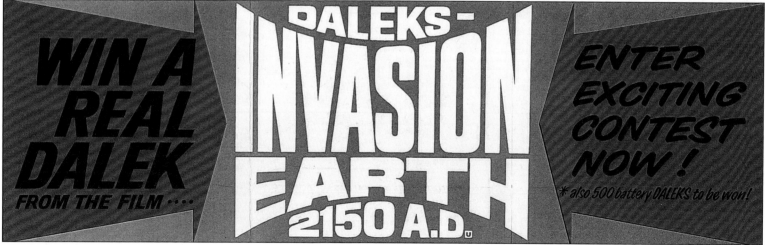

harassing a Dalek on the Dickensian street set. There was an explosion of accompanying promotional items, from posters to banners, serviettes and milk bottle collars. Once again, the Lewis department stores had Dalek displays and celebrity guests, including comedy actress Dora Bryan. Full-size cardboard Daleks were made available to shops and cinemas.

Reviews for the film were mixed, and Peter Cushing himself went on record regarding his treatment at the hands of critics.

He spoke with the *London Evening Standard* on the 3rd March, "A lot of people have accused me of lowering my standards, but I've never felt I'm wasting myself. I've kept working. And surely that's the most important thing."

The Daleks went to New York again, and there was a photocall by the iconic Empire State Building. Back in the UK, the film opened again at Studio One in London on 22nd July before going on general release on 5th August. The

THIS PAGE: Win a Dalek competition advertisements. Photos from Richard Holliss.

novelty value of Daleks in colour and on the big screen was not enough to shield the ears of cinema-goers from hostile critics. Box office takings were lower and comments harsher the second time around. *The Morning Star* described the desolate futuristic London setting as looking "like leftovers from an old film about the London Blitz." The film was paired as a double feature with lesser films such as the Western drama *Indian Paint* (1965).

There were, though, supporters of the film's ambitious attempt to create higher production values for *Doctor Who*, with more realism than anything seen on television or in the previous film.

"This second Dalek story has none of the slapstick comedy of the first and gains by it. Fast-moving direction and impressive special effects" – *Kine Weekly* 14th July 1966

"Flemyng keeps things moving, throwing plenty of action and explosion in for good measure." – *Films and Filming* September 1966

"A lot more style and polish than its predecessor. Just the job for the holiday season!" – *Daily Cinema*

"The sets are quite an eyeful, so are the special effects, and director Gordon Flemyng can teach Disney a lot about packing in the action." – Alexander Walker, *London Evening Standard*

Subotsky was philosophical about the film's performance: "The selling point of the original film was that it was in colour and on the big screen. By the second film we had done all this, so really it was just another film. It wasn't as successful as the first film, and I didn't think it would be. In fact, I suggested that we didn't make it, but frankly, I think it turned out to be a better picture than the first one."

REAL DALEKS TO BE WON! SEE BACK OF PACK

from the film 'Daleks—Invasion Earth, 2150 AD'

It's a long way to push a DALEK

Ten-year-old John Streeter won this Dalek in a 'Sugar Puffs Win A Real Dalek' competition organised by Quaker Oats Ltd. for the film "Daleks — Invasion Earth 2150 A.D." He was presented with his formidable prize at ABC's Astoria Cinema, Brighton, and here we see him outside the cinema starting to push the Dalek home. But as John lived 25 miles away, the journey was actually accomplished by van.

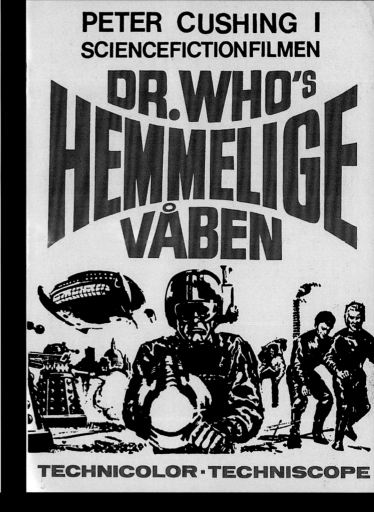

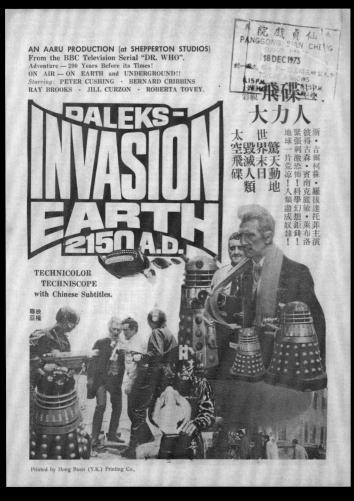

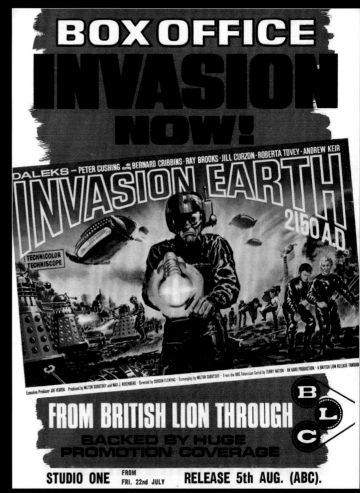

THE LOST RADIO ADVENTURE

An abridged version of the film soundtracks was heard on BBC Radio for several years. Then, on Friday 18th November 1966 at 7.30 pm, the BBC Radio Light Programme Movietime broadcast a cut-down version of twenty-seven minutes of audio from the film, with linking narration. Stanmark Productions Ltd and Watermill Productions created this. A further pilot of a new drama is said to have been recorded with Peter Cushing. *Journey into Time* would have seen Dr. Who and Susan transported to the American Revolution. The recording was never broadcast and is believed lost.

The film would receive its British television première on BBC1 on Saturday 19th August 1972 at 7.05 pm. The ratings for the sequel would top the first Dalek film that premièred the previous month on BBC1, with viewing figures of 10.7 million making it the most watched *Doctor Who* since 1965.

OPPOSITE TOP LEFT: Spanish Rosa Films Distributor half sheet poster. Photo from Christopher Hill / The Space Museum.

OPPOSITE TOP RIGHT: Norwegian Promo Flyer. Photo from Christopher Hill / The Space Museum.

OPPOSITE BOTTOM LEFT: Chinese full-page advertisement. Photo from Mick Hall.

OPPOSITE BOTTOM RIGHT: British Lion Distributor preview poster. Photo from Richard Holliss.

BELOW: Promotional art created by Stanmark Productions.

LOST IN TIME – THE THIRD DR. WHO FILM

BELOW: Mechanoids built by Shawcraft Models. Filming for 'The Chase' took place at Riverside Studios from April to June 1965 and would include a brief appearance from a pair of movie Daleks.

The poor box office reception to *Invasion Earth* compared to the first Dalek feature caused plans for a third film to be shelved. It was intended to be another adaptation of a Terry Nation television serial, 'The Chase', first broadcast on 22 May 1965. The serial was six episodes long and set on several planets and time periods. The Daleks are in pursuit of the Doctor to take control of his TARDIS. This series showcased Nation's newest mechanical creations: the Mechanoids, hoping to relight the fire of Dalekmania.

These spherical robots, the Mechanoids, were created by humans to complete dangerous and manual tasks in colonising other worlds. When the Mechanoids are abandoned, they unite for their survival, calling their home planet Mechanus. Once they become enemies of the Daleks, the stage is set for a metal-on-metal face off. Unfortunately, the Mechanoids would only appear in the last two episodes. Like the Daleks, creating the practical full-size machines would fall to in-house BBC designer

Raymond Cusick, who chose a geodesic design for their domed, flame-throwing rivals. Ironically, two feature film Daleks did make a final brief appearance in 'The Chase' in 1965.

Cast member Roberta Tovey would have been happy to reprise her role as Susan for the second time. "When we were doing the second film, rumours were going around that they were thinking of doing a third. But that was as far as it ever got to me. I didn't hear any more. And so they just decided against it. I think, as they say, the second one wasn't as successful as the first one. I think they just lost interest in it, and Peter Cushing was engaged to do other things after that.

"I had always hoped they would do another one, because we were just beginning. The first film was our first adventure – we were making the machine work the first time. The second film was just the second adventure for us. I don't know why they didn't actually get to make a third one."

Over the years, Subotsky kept the dream of a third film alive, with a plan for a *Doctor Who* film in the 1970s starring Tom Baker. In Richard Holliss' 1984 interview with Subotsky for *Doctor Who Monthly*, there was even talk of an ambitious big-screen return for the Doctor with director Walter Hill taking the directing reins.

By 1990, Subotsky went further and proved his ambitions for *Doctor Who* were more fantastic than ever. "I already had a screenplay written for a third, but we never got the rights. It's a giant monsters film, and I call it Doctor Who's Greatest Adventure. It's got two Doctors in it, one old and a younger one. I would use Jon Pertwee or Tom Baker for the older Doctor, and anyone good enough could play the younger one. I included two Doctors because the problem is so big, it needs two Time Lords to solve it. This one is a big, big film. I would think upwards of £15 million budget." Subotsky intended to repurpose an existing non-Dr. Who horror script for this, entitled *King Crab*.

DR. WHO & THE DALEKS : THE OFFICIAL STORY OF THE FILMS

SIGNING OFF

OPPOSITE: The Doctor and the Dalek pondering a third adventure? Photo from Mick Hall.

BELOW: Susie waves goodbye to the Thals on Skaro.

RIGHT: Dr. Who taking a time and motion study of the Daleks at work. Photo from Mick Hall.

Peter Cushing lamented the further adventures which were planned but never realised. "We came very close to a third and possibly a fourth film. Sadly it didn't come to pass."

Despite the harsh views of critics, both professional and armchair, Cushing embraced this role that brought him to a new generation. "Children just love the Doctor. It is one of the most heroic and successful parts an actor could play. That's no doubt one of the many reasons this series has had such a long run on television. I shall always be grateful for having been a small part of such a success story."

Dr Fiona Subotsky shared with me her view on her husband Milton's place in cinema history. "His central role in the making of the films was not understood in the USA. He found the stories, engaged with the authors, often wrote the scripts, and did the budgets and schedules. He took a very active role in the cutting room. He loved stories of the kind suitable for children, where bad ends come only to villains, and claimed his films were not gory (which was not altogether true). Perhaps it is because they are so clearly 'his' that the films remain of interest."

ABOVE: Peter Cushing publicity portrait image from 1965.

ABOVE RIGHT: William Hartnell on the TARDIS set at Lime Grove Studio D on 17th January 1964 for the serial, 'The Edge of Destruction'. Colourisation by Clayton Hickman.

OPPOSITE TOP: A final goodbye from Cushing's Doctor and companions at the end of *Invasion Earth*.

OPPOSITE BOTTOM: Jennie Linden and Roy Castle in a publicity photo from 1965, reading *TV 21 Magazine*.

Milton Subotsky achieved something no other filmmaker has: putting *Doctor Who* on the big screen. Numerous attempts by studios, large and small, floundered over the years. None found the unique mix of story, cast and timing; lightning in a bottle, which Subotsky captured twice. However, from their mid-1960s screenings to the present day, interest has remained high. Quality toy replicas and a series of costly film restorations attest to both a commercial incentive and a public appetite for these films. The latest incarnation from StudioCanal is a 4k ultra-high resolution version. The original camera negative will be scanned for the first time to produce a faithful and meticulous restoration more akin to a David Lean epic than a medium-budget British family science fiction film from 1965.

The enormous popularity of *Doctor Who* on television through the 1970s and 1980s kept the Peter Cushing films alive, and they have grown in stature with each new generation of film critics. The two Dr. Who films are a testament to the craft of British filmmaking and an American who knew there would be an appetite for big-screen adventures of this uniquely British institution in the making.

By the series' relaunch in 2005, the children of the 1960s were now at the controls of power for the television series. The echoes of their love for the Subotsky films reverberate throughout the many new incarnations of the Doctor. Both films set impossibly high production standards for television to compete with. In 2010 the controversial on-screen debut of the 'New Paradigm' Daleks demonstrated design parallels with their big-screen cousins. The film's original TARDIS romance between Barbara and Ian would be a first for *Who* fans and would not be seen again until companions Rory and Amy joined the 11th Doctor Matt Smith in 2010.

With audiences more accepting of a changing leading actor in part, invidious comparisons between Cushing and Hartnell have faded over the years. Like John Hurt's War Doctor in 2013, we can consider the Cushing incarnation as existing in an alternative universe where he sits reading his latest edition of Eagle Comic.

Fans and the press questioned his *Doctor Who* roles, but Cushing reflected fondly on the role later in his career. "I had played Winston Smith in *Nineteen Eighty-Four* on television, and the next thing I played Doctor Who. I was doing it in the cinema while Bill Hartnell was doing it on TV! That's the way it goes. It was no surprise to me to learn that the first *Doctor Who* film was in the top twenty box office hits of 1965, despite the panning the critics gave us. That's why they made the sequel and why they spent twice as much money on it. Those films are among my favourites because they brought me popularity with younger children. They'd say their parents didn't want to meet me in a dark alley, but *Doctor Who* changed that."

BIBLIOGRAPHY

DVDs / VIDEOS

Dalek Commentary – StudioCanal
Dalekmania – StudioCanal
Doctor Who: 'Death to the Daleks' – BBC Video
A Whole Scene Going – BBC Television, 16th March
1966, prod. Elizabeth Cowley

BOOKS

Peter Cushing: A Life in Film – David Miller (Titan Books, 2013)
*Freddie Francis: The Straight Story from Moby Dick
to Glory, a Memoir* – Freddie Francis (Scarecrow Press 2013)
Doctor Who: The Sixties – David J. Howe, Mark Stammers
& Stephen James Walker (Virgin Publishing 1993)
Doctor Who: A Celebration – Peter Haining (WH Allen & Co., 1983)
*Now on the Big Screen: The Unofficial and Unauthorised Guide to Doctor Who
at the Movies* – Charles Norton (Telos Publishing, 2015)

MAGAZINES

Doctor Who Magazine 145 & 469
Doctor Who Monthly 84
Cinefantastique vol. 2 issue 4
Starburst 6
Doctor Who Bulletin 81

ONLINE ARTICLES

Milton Subotsky obituary – *The Guardian*
Dr. Who Interviews – *drwhointerviews.wordpress.com*
Shawcraft Models – *ProjectDalek.co.uk*
Matte Shot: A Tribute to Golden Era Special FX –
nzpetesmatteshot.blogspot.com

MUSIC

Dr. Who & The Daleks Soundtrack CD – Silva Screen Records

ACKNOWLEDGEMENTS

THANKS TO

Andrew Boyle
Anthony Clark
Anthony Martyn Clark
Anthony Waye
Bernard Cribbins
Bryan Hands
Character Options
Chris Achilléos
Christopher Hill – The Space Museum
www.thespacemuseum.net
Clayton Hickman
Colin Young
David J. Howe
David Stoner – Silva Screen Records
Dee Constable
Derek Handley

Dr Fiona Subotsky
Emil Fortune – Titan Books
Frank Gallaugher – Titan Books
William Robinson – Titan Books
Graham Humphreys
Ian Wheeler – Doctor Who Appreciation Society
Jason Flemyng
Jennie Linden
Jeremy Aspinall
Jill Curzon
John Darley / Project Dalek
Mark Wolf
Massimo Moretti – STUDIOCANAL
Michael Bloomfield – The Tom Chantrell Archive
Mick Hall
Mike Purver

Nick Landau
Orlando Arocena
Peter Sims
Ray Brooks
Richard Holliss
Robert Davidson – Davidson Auctions
Roberta Tovey
Scott Goodman
Simon Ward
Steve Walker – Product Enterprise
Sarah Sorkin – Prop Store
Tim Lawes – Prop Store
Tim Doyle
Toby Chamberlain
Tony Jordan – Doctor Who Appreciation Society
Vivian Cheung